Lash LaRue,

King of the Bullwhip

by

Chuck Thornton

and

David Rothel

Published by:

Empire Publishing, Inc.
PO Box 717
Madison, NC 27025-0717

Phone: 336-427-5850 • Fax: 336-427-7372
www.empirepublishinginc.com

Lash LaRue, King of the Bullwhip by Chuck Thornton and David Rothel

Portions of *Lash LaRue, King of the Bullwhip* were published in a limited edition in 1986 under the title *The Western Adventures of Lash LaRue.*

ISBN Number 0-944019-06-4
Library of Congress Catalog Card Number 88071610

Manufactured in the United States of America

First Printing: 1988
Second Printing: 2003
1 2 3 4 5 6 7 8 9

Contents

Acknowledgments

Dedication

"Everlasting Peace"

A Word from the Publisher

1 Lash LaRue, King of the Bullwhip by David Rothel 10

2 The King of the Bullwhip Answers His Fans' Questions by David Rothel 36

3 The Western Adventures of Lash LaRue by Chuck Thornton 62

Song of Old Wyoming 63
The Caravan Trail 64
Wild West 65
Law of the Lash 67
Border Feud 69
Pioneer Justice 71
Ghost Town Renegades 73
Return of the Lash 75
The Fighting Vigilantes 79
Cheyenne Takes Over 83
Stage to Mesa City 85
Dead Man's Gold 90
Mark of the Lash 95
Frontier Revenge 97
Outlaw Country 100
Son of Billy the Kid 104
Son of a Badman 106
King of the Bullwhip 111
The Daltons' Women 113
The Thundering Trail 117
The Vanishing Outpost 119
The Black Lash 121
The Frontier Phantom 123

4 From the Pages of Lash's Scrapbook 128

Selected Bibliography 157

About the Authors 158

Acknowledgments

The authors acknowledge with appreciation the help of the following organizations and individuals in the preparation of the book: Tommy Williamson, Phil Smoot, Mitchell Schaperkotter, Charles Sharpe, Boyd Magers, Bob Kenney, Clyde and Juanita Carroll, Frank Alcord, The Shannon Press, Jim Rutland, and Film Favorites.

We want to especially thank the following individuals for the photographs included in this publication: Grady Franklin, Tom Wyatt, Les Leverett, Howard Moore, Ralph Spicer, Franklin Knowles, and Packy Smith.

We are deeply indebted to Dana Cox (who may be Lash's biggest fan) for his special interest and contributions.

To our "pack rat" buddy, Sammy Fulp, thanks for saving all those valuable newspaper clippings, photographs, and other materials we used to enhance the Lash LaRue story.

Great appreciation goes to Rhonda Lemons and Doneen Key of Empire Publishing for overseeing the production and distribution of this book.

And, of course, special thanks goes to the man himself — Lash LaRue.

DEDICATED

to

"King of the Bullwhip,"

Lash LaRue

EVERLASTING PEACE

I watched a sleeping city
From the crest of a sloping hill
In the cold, gray light of morning
While everything was still.

And as I watched, my thoughts
Were not
Of the beauty that
Lay at hand;

They wandered to death,
Destruction, Despair —
To a torn and bleeding
Land.

Most of us have much the
same passions,
No matter what language we speak
All of us have the same want
For life and to find the
Happiness we seek.

I dream of a world
That knows no hate
With a faith in God
Designed so great

Aggression and intolerance
Would have no place
And all men are equal
Regardless of Race.

I know some day
We all will see
A world at peace
In tranquility

When men shall find
The time again
To voice a praise to God and
Then
Man's right to Life and Liberty
would never cease
And the world would find
An Everlasting Peace.

Conceived and written
by Lash LaRue

A Word from the Publisher

I first became aware of Lash LaRue in the year 1947, when my local theatre suddenly was bombarded with Western movies starring a fairly new cowboy dressed in black from head to toe and wielding a bullwhip.

During 1947, Lash starred in eight pictures, and I believe our little movie house played all of them. Those eight pictures, produced by PRC Pictures and Eagle Lion, launched a career for the original "man in black" that would cause him to be recognized and well known for his entire life. After all, who could forget the name Lash LaRue? I never knew anyone named Lash until I saw it come blazing across the silver screen bigger than life.

There is much to be said about this man who today is one of the best remembered movie cowboys who ever rode a horse and went that-a-way. Again—it's the name, the man, or perhaps a mixture of both that causes us to remember Lash LaRue. One night, while watching *The Tonight Show*, Johnny Carson was conversing with guest Lewis Grizzard, and the subject got around to Western movies. Grizzard quickly mentioned three cowboys that he remembered: Tom Mix, Gene Autry, and Lash LaRue. This scene is repeated time and time again via television, radio, magazines, movies, and newspapers on a quite regular basis. I repeat, Lash has made his mark in the pages of lasting time.

Another time while watching the television program *Hell Town* from a few years back, Robert Blake, in character as a priest, was talking to God, and in his conversation blurted out, ". . . and God, please bless all the ole cowboys like Gene Autry, Roy Rogers, and Lash LaRue." Once more, the Lash LaRue magic surfaced.

You are holding in your hands our book on the original "man in black," Lash LaRue. Both Johnny Cash and Waylon Jennings declare they wear black clothing due to watching Lash on the screen while they were young men growing up. We at Empire are grateful to Chuck Thornton and David Rothel for writing this book that will allow this generation and future generations the opportunity to remember this legendary celebrity.

Chapter 1

Lash LaRue, King of the Bullwhip

by David Rothel

To start with, Lash LaRue was an enigma—a puzzling, contradictory, show business phenomena. He never fit the cowboy hero mold, yet he was a star of Western films for several years. His off-screen adventures over the years commanded far more interest, but he ducked questions about his personal past like (as one interviewer put it) "an old gunfighter dodging bullets." And would you believe that this former silver-screen cowboy was a poet of considerable skill and sensitivity? Well, he was, as many film festival fans will attest, but more about that later.

Yes, he was an enigma. Item: Among Lash's twenty-some Western films from the 1940s and '50s, there are very few that Western film critics and aficionados identify as quite good, and yet his films were very popular with the public when they were originally released, and they are remembered fondly more than fifty years later by fans.

Item: Lash was a sinister-voiced, sulky-looking Western film hero clad in black (from Stetson to boot) at a time when white-hatted, gaudily-dressed singing cowboys ruled the Hollywood celluloid range, and yet the power of his screen presence in his first Western, ***Song of Old Wyoming,*** brought forth bags of fan mail—some say equal to those for Gene Autry and Roy Rogers. One writer commented that Lash's screen smile "reminded you of a prohibition racketeer who had just heard that his crosstown rival had turned up in concrete shoes." Nevertheless, the fans loved him and made him a star.

Item: Lash wouldn't talk about any of his personal "bad jazz," as he called it, from the past—many broken marriages, financial problems, several brushes with the law—but this born-again Christian would speak movingly and inspirationally to church congregations and civic groups—the pillars of the community—and quote the Bible and discuss religion in general by the hour.

Item: Lash often talked like a side-of-the-mouth carnie barker making his you-ain't-seen-nothing-yet pitch to the customers, but he could turn mellow-voiced as he movingly recited a melancholy poem conjured from his own nimble mind. From what well of words within did this mesmerizer draw his inspiration? He was not explaining anything. "You figure it out," he seemed to be saying as his dark eyes took in your perplexity. Yes, he was an enigma, to be sure.

Though he was reticent to respond candidly about his personal life's roller coaster ride, his poetry spoke volumes about this gentle, complex human being. Suggesting a sensitiveness about the down side of his past, Lash opened one poem by quoting rap comedian Lord Buckley: "The bad jazz a man blows lives long after he's cut out. And the good things he might do are forgotten with his face."

His poetic mood could turn sentimentally romantic, as in the poem where he conjured

Al "Lash" LaRue in a publicity pose from Universal Studios, 1944.

a "dream girl" who would share a love with him that "will withstand all sorrows and strife."

A world-weary, hurting, and used Lash acknowledged in another poem that he had been "kicked around, pushed and shoved," that "he'd had enough!" But then in his gentlest mien he advised that if you want something from him, "ask me nice; just ask me nice."

In still another of his poems he proudly, defiantly proclaimed that "it's better to be the bastard son of love than legitimate SOB." Once after reciting the poem for an appreciative audience, Lash murmured in a sotto-voice aside, "And that's about the story of my life."

Then in his "Everlasting Peace" poem, Lash's thoughts turned to "a torn and bleeding land," and he dreamed of "a world that knows no hate," where "men will find the time again to voice a praise to God."

Yes, Lash LaRue was an enigma.

Even Alfred LaRue's birth date and place are shrouded in confusion. One source says he was born on March 5, 1921; others say June 14, 15, or 16, 1917. (Lash wouldn't talk about his age in specifics. He did say, "Age is a psychological trap. If I started thinking about how old I am, I wouldn't be able to get up in the morning." By the way, he hated the name Al or Alfred because he felt that it sounded like the name of a gangster or worse.) One source indicates that his mother gave birth to him in Michigan; another proclaims Chicago, Illinois; still another assures us it was Gretna, Louisiana. Most sources agree that he grew up in Gretna with his mother.

Lash's father, reportedly a traveling hotel representative and real estate operator, died when Al was very young. "I never had a daddy," Lash once said in an interview. "I was a widow's son. She kept looking for a man to help me, and I'd run them out. I didn't want them around. So the only one I had to look up to was people like John Wayne... We met many times. We didn't get as well acquainted as I'd like to have, I wrote him a letter when he was in the hospital, and I told him I never knew my dad, but if I had, I'd wish my dad had been a lot like him."

By the time he reached high school age, Al had managed to journey to California where he attended St. John's Military Academy in Los Angeles, from which he graduated. Later he enrolled at College of the Pacific in Stockton, California, where, among other things, he took up drama to overcome a speech impediment. It is unclear whether he graduated from college. Some sources say yes; others indicate he only spent three years at Stockton and never realized his dream of becoming a lawyer.

Whatever the situation was, after leaving college he worked at a variety of jobs—real estate salesman, even hair dresser, it has been reported. It was while he was attempting to sell real estate that he met screen actor George Brent, who saw something in young LaRue and arranged a screen test for him at Warner Brothers Studio. Perhaps because of his likeness to Humphrey Bogart, a contract star at Warner's, Al was rejected by the studio.

LaRue's thirst for show business had been whetted by his screen test at Warner's, so he started knocking on doors at other studios. Universal turned out to be his lucky studio, and soon he was playing small roles in several pictures, among them a couple of Deanna

Lash made his first appearance in a Western film in *Song of Old Wyoming* which starred Eddie Dean. Lash played The Cheyenne Kid, a good guy gone wrong. In the above lobby card, Lash is engaged in a shootout from his vantage point behind some barrels.

Durbin pictures—***Christmas Holiday*** (1944) and ***Lady on a Train*** (1945). The first time he was really noticed in a film occurred when he was cast as Migsy, a rough street kid, in ***The Master Key*** (1945), a thirteen-chapter Universal serial. Milburn Stone and Dennis Moore were the main actors; Al was listed eleventh in the cast.

Al's big movie break came in 1945 when he was cast as The Cheyenne Kid in the Eddie Dean starrer ***Song of Old Wyoming***. Cheyenne is a ne'er do-well who discovers late in the picture that he is the long-lost son of harried ranch woman Ma Conway (Sarah Padden). He switches to the side of the good guys just in time to stop a bullet and die.

It was in ***Song of Old Wyoming*** that Lash introduced the whip. Although most people who saw the film vividly remember Al's use of the bullwhip, it was actually only used twice in the picture—at the mid point and again at the final shoot-out. It is not even seen at other times, but audiences picked up on the whip and were enthralled by it.

The fans loved the black-clad figure of The Cheyenne Kid and sent bags of fan mail to PRC Pictures, the production company, stating that they wanted to see more of the man in black—the cowboy who cracked the whip. PRC was happy to oblige.

Lash was next cast in ***Caravan Trail*** (1946), another Eddie Dean musical Western. Since he had been killed off as The Cheyenne Kid in ***Song of Old Wyoming***, he had to return as a new character. This time he was Cherokee, the leader of a two-man gang of comic outlaws. His bumbling henchmen were played by Charlie King and Black Jack O'Shea. Cherokee and his buddies helped Eddie bring the outlaws to justice, and he got to live at the end of the picture. The most startling thing about viewing the film today is the discovery that Lash ***never*** touches a whip in the picture! As in ***Song of Old Wyoming***, he steals the picture (except for when Eddie Dean sings "Wagon Wheels").

Lash was sometimes criticized for his acting in the films, but a look-see at any of his early pictures reveals that he had a good screen voice and handled himself very capably in the acting department—certainly better than many B-Western film thespians. His horseback riding seemed a bit tentative at times in the early films, but he looked good in the fight scenes before the stunt double took over for the really rough-and-tumble stuff. In some cases Lash handled all of the fighting himself!

The last of Lash's apprentice work in Eddie Dean pictures was in ***Wild West*** (1946), in which he played a character named Stormy Day. He, Eddie Dean, and Roscoe Ates (the

Eddie Dean points the way to adventure for Lash and Roscoe Ates in this scene from Wild West.

Lash's co-star in all of his Westerns was Al "Fuzzy" St. John. A Keystone cop in silent pictures, St. John later made a career for himself playing sidekick for a number of Western stars including Fred Scott, Bob Steele, Don Barry, George Houston, and Buster Crabbe.

comic sidekick) were a three-some in the picture not unlike The Three Mesquiteers over at Republic Pictures. Lash found his whip again for this picture and used it effectively to thwart the owlhoots.

As a result of the impressive showings Lash made in the Eddie Dean films and a need to fill the void created by the ending of the Buster Crabbe Western series in 1946, PRC decided to create a new Western film star they would call "Lash" LaRue. The studio assigned Buster's old sidekick, Al "Fuzzy" St John, to assist their debuting whip-wielding hero.

In a strange bit of character juggling, the studio decided that in the series Lash should play a U.S. Marshal named Cheyenne Davis or, informally, The Cheyenne Kid. Never mind that in ***Song of Old Wyoming*** The Cheyenne Kid had been an outlaw and was killed off at the end of the picture. As the series progressed, Lash was mostly referred to as Cheyenne Davis. Author Buck Rainey (in an article on Lash) speculated that "some government bureaucrat in finance probably balked at honoring a payroll voucher made out to The Cheyenne Kid."

"Slashing a *NEW* thrill trail across the old West" proclaimed the posters for the first entry in the series, ***Law of the Lash*** (1947). Lash's first starring vehicle was a financial success and was followed by seven more episodes during that same year—***Border Feud, Pioneer Justice, Ghost Town Renegades, Return of the Lash, The Fighting Vigilantes, Cheyenne Takes Over***, and ***Stage to Mesa City***. With that the PRC series ended—just one long year of furious activity!

The casts of the films were composed of popular B-Western regulars such as George Chesebro, Lane Bradford, Marshall Reed, Steve Clark, Jennifer Holt, Russell Arms (later of *Your Hit Parade* on television), John Merton, Bob Woodward, Budd Buster, Nancy Gates, and Terry Frost. From a quality standpoint the series was run-of-the mill, but it could be argued that ***Border Feud*** and ***Cheyenne Takes Over*** were a cut above the others—but that's only one Western film critic's opinion. The weakest entry in the series was probably the last, ***Stage to Mesa City***. Stock footage from previous episodes and long, aimless riding sequences slowed the film to a snail's pace. The PRC series was produced by Jerry Thomas and directed by long-time B-Western helmsman, Ray Taylor.

In addition to the Western series Lash did for PRC in 1947, he also appeared in two melodramas for the company. ***Heartaches***, a nifty little murder story, starred Chill Wills in the unlikely role of a crooner/murderer. Lash, billed as Al LaRue, had a small role. The other film was ***The Enchanted Valley***, released in 1948. In it Lash played Trigger Malloy, a gangster.

In 1948 a new film company called Western Adventure Productions was established by producer Ron Ormond for the purpose of filming a new Western series starring Lash LaRue. ***Dead Man's Gold*** started the series off and was quickly followed by ***Mark of the Lash, Frontier Revenge***, ***Outlaw Country, Son of Billy the Kid***, and ***Son of a Badman***. Starting with this series, Lash played Lash LaRue. As in the PRC series, all of the films were directed by veteran Ray Taylor. In addition to producing, Ron Ormond wrote all but one of the original stories with associate producer Ira Webb. Director Taylor wrote ***Frontier Revenge***.

This first series for Western Adventure Productions was on a par with the PRC se-

Sony Home Video packaged five of Lash's films in the above design. The films are *Cheyenne Takes Over, Ghost Town Renegades, Border Feud, Return of the Lash,* and *Stage to Mesa City.*

ries—no better, no worse. It was very apparent to the discerning eye that no money was being wasted on the series. The sets were skimpy, as were the number of people in the casts. There was a feeling about the films of being rushed, and according to Lash they were. As Lash said many times about the filming of these pictures, "If the director could see it and hear it, he said to print it."

But this situation was true of many B Westerns by the late 1940s. Film production costs were escalating, television was arriving on the scene, and the post-war American pub-

As this studio publicity photo shows, the camera was kind to this up-and-coming Western movie star.

Lash and Fuzzy pause in front of the famous rocks at Iverson's Ranch, a favorite location for shooting B Westerns. *Dead Man's Gold* was the first of the Western Adventure Productions released by Screen Guild.

lic was beginning to be more discriminating in its choice of entertainment fare. Most B films—Western or otherwise—were drawing fewer and fewer patrons. Republic Studio, the leading producer of B Westerns was slashing budgets, cutting back on the number of pictures, and working with smaller casts. A gang that would have included eight to ten outlaws only a few years before, now had only three or four law-breakers terrorizing the countryside. Only Gene Autry over at the Columbia Studio was grinding out expensive B Westerns as if they would go on forever. Forever, as it turned out, was 1953, when all B-Western production ceased.

The casts in the first Western Adventure Productions series were composed of many B-Western favorites. Popular leading lady Peggy Stewart was in two of them. Villains, sheriffs, and bartenders were essayed by popular character actors such as Terry Frost, John Cason, Pierce Lyden, Lane Bradford, Marshall Reed, Britt Wood, Tom London, Jim Bannon, George Chesebro, Bud Osborne, John Merton, Dan White, and others. Noel Neill, TV Superman's Lois Lane, was Lash's leading lady in ***Son of a Badman*** (1949).

Outlaw Country (1949) stood out in Lash's mind as one of his favorites from this series because he got to play a double role—Lash and his fugitive twin brother, The Frontier

Phantom. The posters screamed, "It's Loaded with Dynamite...Twin Brothers...One the Law, One the Outlaw." Apparently the producers must have been pleased with the picture too, because three years later a Lash starrer entitled ***The Frontier Phantom*** (1952) was released. The film was mostly ***Outlaw Country*** told in money-saving flashback with only a few minutes of new film serving primarily as a wrap-around for the old footage.

Lash's final series bore the credits "J. Francis White, Jr. and Joy Houck present..." followed by the film title and then Lash and Fuzzy's names. Regardless of who was "presenting," the films were still coming out of the Western Adventure Productions store with Ron Ormond producing and now directing—likely a cost-saving device. Realart took over the distribution of the films.

King of the Bullwhip (1951), the first film in the last series, is the main picture that LaRue fans speak of when discussing Lash's best work. The film is the standard B-Western fare, but the climatic whip fight between Lash and the bandit El Azote is certainly memorable—maybe partly so because one doesn't see whip fights very often. The two opponents

Lash had plenty of opportunity to crack his famous whip in *Son of Billy the Kid.* Fuzzy St. John must have wondered if he would ever leave the Kid character behind. He had already done two Billy the Kid film series with Bob Steele and Buster Crabbe.

These scenes are from one of Lash's favorite films, *Outlaw Country,* in which he played a dual role.

spar up and around the rocks on the Iverson Ranch movie location for several minutes, creating a considerable amount of edge-of-your-seat action as well as suspense. The fact that Lash takes his licks during the fight helps to build the suspense. There appears to be doubt as to the outcome even though the audience knows that the hero has to succeed in the end. Realizing that they had a winner in the whip fight, the producer decided to get as much mileage out of it as he could. Highlights from the whip fight were also used behind the opening credits of the picture.

King of the Bullwhip also boasts an unusually strong supporting cast including Jack Holt, Tom Neal, Anne Gwynne, George Lewis, and Dennis Moore. A suspicion of nepotism creeps in as one also notices the names Mary Lou Webb and Willie Houck in the cast. Ira Webb was associate producer and Joy Houck was "presenting" the film.

The next film, ***The Daltons' Women***, is often overlooked as a Lash LaRue film because Lash and Fuzzy are listed fourth and fifth in the cast (Tom Neal, Pamela Blake, and Jack Holt are top-billed), and the title certainly doesn't suggest a B Western. The poster art for the film is definitely not your usual B-Western escapist fare. The searing quote at the top of the poster threatens, "FOR MY MAN...I'D KILL YOU!...OR HIM." Accompanying this vow are photos of several vivacious women (Daltons', of course) joyfully struggling with little success to keep the tops of their gowns from exposing their ample bosoms. This was an all-new, rather unexpected advertising ploy for the pre-pubescent Saturday matinee crowd. By conservative 1951 standards, the film advertising had the appearance of a soft-core porno movie. But that was before you bought your ticket. Once inside the theater, it became clear that this was just a streamlined Lash LaRue Western.

The other four pictures in this last series appeared to be filmed using mostly left-over and reused footage from all of the other films made by Western Adventure Productions. Their titles were ***The Thundering Trail, The Vanishing Outpost, The Black Lash,*** and the before-mentioned film, ***The Frontier Phantom***. There was probably little more than fifteen minutes of new footage shot for each of these four films. ***The Frontier Phantom*** was released in February of 1952, a time when B films in general were succumbing to the last death-rattle gasp in the face of television's onslaught. The Western film career of Lash LaRue ended with this film. In his wildest dreams Lash could never have guessed that his films would remain popular in television reruns, at Western film festivals, and on home video fifty years after the dust had settled on the last B-Western film.

As so many other Western stars had done when their film careers faded, Lash took to the road, appearing in rodeos, fairs, wild West shows, carnivals, and theaters where his films were still playing—in short, anywhere he could find paying customers for his whip act. And he *was* popular, particularly in the South where his films had always been extremely successful.

During the 1950s Lash appeared in several television series. In *Lash of the West,* produced by J. Francis White and Joy Houck of his last film series, Lash hosted the series and played his own grandson. He introduced his old films as if he were reminiscing about his grandfather who was Lash LaRue of the old West.

When the *Lash of the West* series ended, Lash appeared in several episodes of two Russell Hayden television series, *26 Men* (supposedly true stories of the Arizona Rangers at

Lash and his popular leading lady Peggy Stewart pose for this publicity picture. Peggy was Lash's Western heroine in two films and a villainess in *The Black Lash* (1952).

Lash is seen here with two young fans during a break from filming at Iverson's Ranch. Notice the Lash LaRue T-shirts the boys are wearing.

the turn of the century starring Tris Coffin and Kelo Henderson) and *The Adventures of Judge Roy Bean* (exploits of the judge who made the law west of the Pecos starring Edgar Buchanan and Jack Beutel). These were very low-budget shows even for television, and Lash played a variety of roles, though usually villains.

Lash's most notable television role was in the Hugh O'Brian series, *The Life and Legend of Wyatt Earp*. During the 1959 season Lash played Johnny Behan, the crooked sheriff of Tombstone, Arizona, during the time Earp was the marshal. To put it kindly, Lash and Hugh O'Brian did not get along. Since O'Brian was the star of the series, Lash packed up and left. (The reader can get more details of the LaRue/O'Brian brouhaha in the question and answer section of this book.)

After his television years, Lash went on the road again with his Western whip act. But the times they were a'changing, and it wasn't all for the good in Lash's case. "Things began going drastically downhill for me from that time on," Lash said. He finally wound up in Nevada managing a combination restaurant and motel in Reno. He was married at this time to his tenth wife (according to one of his interviews), an excellent horsewoman and a former

Lash LaRue's Western film career ended in 1952. Over fifty years later his films are still being shown on television, at film festivals, and on home video. The principles that Lash refers to in the above dedication are those engendered in the B-Western films.

leading lady of B Westerns, Reno Browne.

It was during this time in his life, the 1960s, that evangelist Bob Woodward visited Reno. "I wasn't too taken with preaching at the time, but I went to see Woodward out of sheer curiosity. I'd heard about a couple of evangelists—Billy Graham and Oral Roberts—who were making the rounds, saving and healing lost souls, so I wondered if Woodward could do the same. And during his sermon, he mentioned something which stuck with me. He said he'd once been a bank president in Chicago. I was born in Chicago (sic), and I figured anyone who once ran a big bank should know plenty about the world, so I paid more attention to what he was saying. The Lord's Spirit moved inside me then, but not quite hard enough."

But Lash did feel an "awakening" within himself and began to speak to church groups as a lay evangelist. According to Lash, his wife Reno thought he was "cracked" when he asked her to join him in spreading God's word. The marriage soon foundered, and Lash hit the road again. "I started giving witness in little churches here and there in Texas, Louisiana, Mississippi...And I set up the Lash LaRue Evangelistic Association, Inc., in Long Beach, California."

My own first-time meeting with Lash was in the early 1970s when he was working with an evangelist named John "3:16" Cook in St. Petersburg, Florida. The 3:16 in John's name referred to the Gospel of St. John: "For God so loved the world, that he gave His only begotten Son, that whosoever believeth in Him should not perish, but have everlasting life." John had founded a mission to work with drunks, drifters, and other derelicts who had reached their end of the trail in St. Pete. During 1973 and '74 Lash assisted John in his mission, provided name value for fund-raising activities, and also was an extremely effective speaker before religious and civic groups in the area.

The promise of an inspirational talk by former cowboy movie star, Lash LaRue, lured me to a Young Republican's meeting at a restaurant in Sarasota, Florida, my home. John 3:16 and several residents from the mission accompanied Lash to the meeting. At that time I only knew Lash from the silver screen, and I was astounded by his ability to deliver a moving, thirty-minute speech/sermon with no notes. After he had finished his talk, I went up and introduced myself, complimented him on his talk, and told him how much I had enjoyed his Western films in years past. He seemed slightly disconcerted by my comment, as though he did not want at that time to be reminded of them—at least that was my impression. A few months later I heard that Lash and John 3:16 had had a falling out and that Lash had moseyed on to new adventures.

As the 1970s crept towards the 1980s, Lash became, as one writer put it, a "celebrity for hire." He made appearances for commercial companies, civic and religious groups, film festivals—you name it—any type of organization that sought his presence. It was a new kind of popularity for Lash. You could find him entertaining his many fans at mobile home distributors, the many nostalgia/Western film festivals held across the country, at car dealerships, horse shows, restaurants, pawn shops, shopping malls, and small retail stores—just to name a few places Lash might turn up.

In 1980 when Iranian militants were holding American hostages in the embassy compound in Tehran, Lash appeared at the Winter Western Film Festival in Memphis, Tennes-

Rocks and more rocks line the hills of Iverson Ranch, a favorite location for shooting Lash LaRue films.

Lash LaRue made many personal appearances during his later years. The above photos, courtesy of Ralph Spicer, were taken at the House of Stars in Madison, NC, in August 1986. At left, Lash signs an autograph for one of his many fans. At right, Lash poses for a photo with Neil Zimmerman, Doneen Key, and fan club president Barbara Arnette.

see. During breakfast with reporter Charles Goodman of the *Press-Scimitar* and some Western fans, Lash commented on the situation in Tehran. “Uncle Sam should be ashamed for letting those Americans stay trapped in the compound,” he exclaimed. Then he drew a parallel to cowboys of the past. “American Cowboys were simple but proud men with strong characters,” Lash said. Regarding the cowboys that were depicted on the movie screens, he added, “Each of those movies had a real moral message. They had high values. And we had better return to those old basic values today, if we know what’s good for us.”

Lash thought for a moment and then turned to one of the fans, “What’s the name of some movie I made which had hostages in it? I made so many I can’t remember what they were all about.” One of the fans said, “There were hostages in ***Outlaw Country***.”

With a nod of the head Lash continued, “Right. In that one the bad guys were holding a man and his beautiful daughter in a kind of Spanish villa. It was out in a remote place somewhere between the United States and Mexico—in a kind of desolate area. I knew what I had to do. I got inside the Spanish castle kind of place, cracked the long bullwhip of mine a few times and straightened some people out—and rescued the man and his daughter.

“People don’t change. This thing in Tehran isn’t new. It’s all happened before in history. This is the same old story only with a different cast. And principles don’t change—those we followed in the old cowboy movies are as good today as they ever were. This nation had better get back to them.”

In the early 1980s Lash sought to reactivate his film career. Using a ploy that Bette

Davis had successfully tried in the 1960s, Lash put an ad in a trade paper asking for work. The ad was noticed by the Associated Press which did a follow-up story with a Lash interview. In May of 1984 it was running in papers throughout the country. Under the headline "Lash Looks for Work," the story was as follows:

> Al "Lash" LaRue, a 1940's cowboy star noted for his all-black garb and expertise with a bullwhip, is hoping to be back in movies again soon.
>
> But, he added Friday, "I'm trying to get away from westerns. There are more opportunities in other pictures."
>
> After a long lapse from the Hollywood scene, LaRue ran an ad in a Hollywood trade paper asking for work in pictures. He says he's now being considered for a part as a college professor in an unidentified picture.

The ad and the Associated Press's pickup of the story apparently worked because in November of that same year the AP had another story out on Lash datelined Asheboro, North Carolina—"Lash LaRue Whips Unemployment":

> Al "Lash" LaRue, star of numerous 1940s cowboy movies, says he's excited about his first major role in over 30 years, in a horror flick that will be filmed in Belews Creek and Kernersville, North Carolina.
>
> Shooting of ***The Dark Power*** is scheduled to begin November 26, said producer and director Phil Smoot of Asheboro, who has worked in various capacities on 24 feature-length motion pictures.
>
> With the exception of a few minor walk-on parts it will be LaRue's first movie role in more than 30 years, and his first in which he isn't playing a cowboy.
>
> "I think that the technical developments in films have been fantastic and I still hold the ambition of eventually directing and producing films," LaRue said.
>
> LaRue's name is perhaps best remembered for the movie ***King of the Bullwhip***, made at a time when LaRue's black outfit, dark demeanor and snapping whip were bywords among fanciers of cowboy films.

Producer/director Phil Smoot and Lash gave an interview to the Raleigh, North Carolina, *News & Observer* in which Smoot said the suspense thriller would have a four-week shooting schedule and a $330,000 budget. Smoot, a graduate of the University of North Carolina at Chapel Hill, commented that he was doing some pre-production work with special effects makeup out of the basement of his Asheboro home.

Lash commented to the reporter that he felt he still had much to offer moviegoers. "Although it may be the afternoon and evening of my life, I feel there is important progress still to be made," Lash told the reporter. He said he liked the idea of Smoot's independently made production because "It's just good to have local people involved in entertainment." Lash stated that he hoped ***The Dark Power*** would be "something I can be proud of" adding that he was often asked which of his films was the best. "I always say that I haven't made it yet," he said jokingly. I have no qualms about going in front of the cameras again. I feel comfortable with an audience, and to me the camera is an audience."

Lash is pictured here on the set of *Dark Power* with the producer/director Phil Smoot and one of the frightening creatures in the film.

Soon after Lash completed ***The Dark Power***, he was once again employed by Phil Smoot for a follow-up film entitled ***Alien Outlaw***. It was also shot in North Carolina in the town of Sparta. Lash's high hopes for the films were somewhat dimmed when they failed to get general distribution in the United States.

In an interview with Phil Smoot, I talked to him about working with Lash LaRue in the two films.

David Rothel: How did you happen to cast Lash in the two movies?

Phil Smoot: You know, some people just have charisma, something which just makes them stand out. Lash is that kind of person. Well, I was working on a movie during the latter part of 1983 in Myrtle Beach, South Carolina. It was a 3-D movie called ***Chain Gang***. As I was working on the film, I noticed a person observing the making of the picture. I said to one of the people on the set, "Who is that guy over there? I haven't seen him before." I was told that it was Lash LaRue.

Lash was there for a couple of weeks. It was suggested that we might be able to get him to do a little part in the film. We never got much of a part for him, but he and I got along really well. I told him that in a year or so I might have the money for a movie and that I would like to use him.

In 1985 we did the film called ***The Dark Power***. You wouldn't believe how little money we had to complete the film. The press release far overstates the amount we had to make the film. The picture has been out on home video, and we haven't made much on it so far. The biggest problem with the film has been the distribution.

The second picture we did with Lash was completed in 1986. It is called ***Alien Outlaw***. I call the movie a comic book movie; ***Superman*** was a comic book movie. I think, if you don't take it seriously, ***Rambo*** is just a comic book movie—if you don't read anything else into it. That's what ***Alien Outlaw*** is. We haven't sold the U.S. home video on it yet because nobody has offered enough money. We are simply going to wait until the money is better. I'm really encouraged by the showing of ***Alien Outlaw***.

David Rothel: Were you familiar with Lash's Western films at the time you first met him at Myrtle Beach?

Lash is seen here on the set for *Dark Power* (1985). The forest ranger's outfit he's wearing is his costume for the film. *(Photo credit: Sammy Fulp)*

Phil Smoot: Quite frankly, I couldn't remember seeing a Lash LaRue film prior to meeting him. Then one day on television I noticed that a film called ***King of the Bullwhip*** was coming on. I watched the picture and was pretty impressed with Lash. Since then I guess I've seen eight or nine of the pictures he was in. The pictures were mostly terrible, but Lash had something about him that you wanted to watch. It's like Boris Karloff. Half the movies he was in are dreadful, but Karloff had a fascination. You really wanted to watch the man. I felt Lash had that. My feeling is that Lash LaRue was probably one of the most wasted performers in screen history. I'm not saying that he was a great actor, but John Wayne wasn't a great actor either. John Wayne was someone you liked to watch on the screen. There was just *something* about John Wayne!

I have always thought since seeing Lash in his films that had he been given the opportunity to be in better productions—films that looked as if they took more than four or five days to shoot—that Lash could really have been big; I mean *really* big! ***King of the Bullwhip*** was probably one of his best films.

David Rothel: How was Lash to work with on the films?

Phil Smoot: Lash was wonderful! I'll be honest with you; when I first started, I was nervous. I had heard stories about all these old cowboy stars being drunks, that you couldn't depend on them, that they wouldn't show up, and that they'd be really awful to deal with. Well, Lash was not only never late, he was always wonderful. He talked to the press, the public, the crew.

I can understand why a man like Lash or Clayton Moore was tough sometimes. They established a reputation over the years of being a character. Lash, Clayton, and a few others made a nice living during their retirement years by making appearances and I can understand why they were protective of their characters. Lash said to me that there was one thing he didn't want me to do. He said, "Don't make me look silly, and don't make me look bad with the whip." Lash was too good with the whip for anybody to make him look bad.

David Rothel: It's obvious that you found Lash as fascinating as the B-Western fans of the 1940s and '50s did.

Phil Smoot: Yes. The guy was quite a fascinating character! You know, Lash *really* touched a lot of people during his career. Any time I mention Lash LaRue to anybody who is over forty, they have a story about a positive experience as a kid with Lash LaRue. I mean, everybody who is over forty met this man! They all have a good memory of this man who came to town.

In the fall of 1984, Lash announced that the well-known artist Learned Hand had completed a painting which he entitled "Lash LaRue, King of the Bullwhip." The 18 by 24-inch painting depicted Lash in three poses—a head and shoulders shot, using the bullwhip, and on his horse Black Diamond. Lash informed his fans that a limited edition printing of 950 copies plus ten artist's proofs were being made available to fans. The prints were reproduced in full color with permanent inks, on acid-free museum stock paper. The artist's proofs, autographed by Lash, were $125 each. The numbered prints were $24.95 autographed by the artist, $34.95 autographed by Lash. Fans of the Western film star found the offering irresistible.

And so Lash LaRue, still dressed in black but with distinguished-looking gray locks

Welcome to the
Lash LaRue Fan Club

Here is a list of pictures from Lash!

Lash LaRue's personal collection is now available on VHS tapes to Fan Club members only! Four of the tapes are in color and fourteen are in black and white. There are others that will be released later. Since these were made thirty years ago, color has changed somewhat. These tapes are the best quality available. Each double feature is a valuable collector's item, and the price is right: just $25.00 for a double feature. Each is signed by Lash with the year recorded. There is value in rarity, so please do not let anyone copy your tape. Some of the ten-cent comic books are now worth over $150.00!

HERE IS A LIST OF THE VIDEO TAPES AVAILABLE THROUGH THE FAN CLUB

Wild West (color) .... *Mark of the Lash (black & white)*
Caravan Trails (color).......... *King of the Bullwhip (black & white)*
Song of Old Wyoming (color).......... *Law of the Lash (black & white)*
Outlaw Country (black & white).......... *Stage to Mesa City (black & white)*
The Frontier Phantom (black & white).......... *Cheyenne Takes Over (black & white)*
Vanishing Outpost (black & white).......... *Border Feud (black & white)*
Dead Man's Gold (black & white).......... *Return of the Lash (black & white)*
Frontier Revenge (black & white).......... *Ghost Town Renegades (black & white)*
Son of Billy the Kid (black & White).......... *Return of the Lash (black & white)*
Please Don't Touch Me (color, not western)
Starring Lash LaRue as a doctor

EACH TAPE LISTED IS MASTERED TO THE ONE ON THE SAME LINE.

Thank you for becoming one of our
Lash LaRue Fans

The $5.00 membership fee is for stamps, etc. You will have first option on future material. We would be happy to hear your suggestions for the Club rules. Please write to

Barbara Arnette
P.O. Box 2484
Sanford, North Carolina 27330

Fan club members received Lash LaRue collectibles as shown here. What fan club member would not be excited to receive a Christmas card like the one above from his hero, Lash LaRue?

and a beard, remained active in the business he had been successful at—the business of show. Show business had not always been good to him, but he had been good for show business. He became a colorful member of the senior-citizen set, and the years mellowed him somewhat. He even remarried—nobody seemed sure what number wife this was. He still loved to talk about his career and to meet his fans—but discussion of his personal life remained off bounds. At film festivals he would sign autographs patiently by the hour. He joked that he did it because he just loved to write his name.

Lash LaRue died on May 21, 1996, in the Providence St. Joseph Medical Center in Burbank, California. The spokesperson for the hospital, adhering to Lash's long penchant for keeping personal things personal, said she could not release any information on the cause of his death.

Ready to hit the fan convention trail, an older Lash poses withthe tools of his trade—rifle, saddle, and trusty bullwhip.

Chapter 2

The King of the Bullwhip Answers His Fans' Questions

by David Rothel

Lash LaRue was a very popular guest at the yearly film festivals held in such cities as Memphis, St. Louis, Charlotte, Atlanta, and Knoxville. For more than a decade he delighted fans with his quick wit, charm, and warm, friendly manner at these soirees.

A popular event at the film festivals is the guest star panel, where several stars field questions thrown by fans in the audience. It has been my pleasure to host/moderate many star panels over the years, and I can attest to the fact that Lash was at his best in the free-wheeling give and take these sessions engendered.

What follows is a compilation of audience questions and Lash's answers that I have audio-taped from as far back as 1980 up to 1987's Charlotte Western Film Fair. In the original panel sessions, of course, there were three or four other guest stars also answering questions, and there was rarely any logical sequential order to the questions, since the questions were drawn randomly from the audience. I have, therefore, arranged the questions from the many panels into a somewhat logical progression until a subject is exhausted. In addition, in the few instances where Lash's panel answer begged more details, I have augmented the answer with a direct quote from a printed interview.

Lash was almost always dressed in his trade-mark black outfit for these occasions. His hair was no longer inky black to match the costume; it was salt and pepper—with emphasis on the salt. His voice was deep and resonant, but the years that added a few creases to his features, gave his voice a honeyed mellowness that tended to lure the audience in his direction. Take it away, Lash!

Lash LaRue and author David Rothel posed for this photo just before the 1983 guest star panel at the Charlotte Film Fair. Rothel hosted the panel and Lash appeared as a guest.

Q - How did you get your start in show business?

A - I went to the College of the Pacific where I studied dramatics because I had a very bad speech impediment. (Lash had a lisp and hesitation stammer, both of which he was able to overcome.) Through a teacher, I met George Brent, a big picture actor at that time. He got me started; in fact, he was responsible for my first film contract. He introduced me to the people at Universal Studios, and I was put under contract.

*   *   *

Q -What was it like to work at Universal in the mid 1940s?

A - Well, I worked on pictures I don't even remember the names of. I was a stock player there. I first worked with Milburn Stone and Dennis Moore in a serial called ***The Master Key.*** The first day there Sarah Padden (a fine character actress of the period) came running across the set and said, "Are you related to Bogart?"
I said, "No."
She said, "Did your mother ever know Bogart?" (audience laughter)
I said, "What are you trying to say, Sarah?" (audience laughter)

* * *

Lash does, indeed, look like Humphrey Bogart, especially when he is in a modern suit.

Q -Critics and audiences have always noted your resemblance to Humphrey Bogart. How do you react to that comparison?

A - Oh, it's silly. I have a lot more hair than Bogart had! (audience laughter) I'm very proud of being compared with Bogart, because I thought he was a fine actor. I don't mind, really, but I *did* have more hair than he.

* * *

Q -What were your feelings when you saw yourself on the screen for the first time?

A - I always thought I was better looking! (audience laughter) The only way I could recognize myself was that I knew nobody else would have bought a sport coat like the one I was wearing. I had a wild check coat on for my test at Universal. Deanna Durbin liked the test, so I got my contract at Universal.

* * *

Q -Weren't you and Deanna Durbin linked romantically for a time?

A - She and I almost.... If it hadn't been for my stupid agent, she and I probably would've been in love. We were very close. She needed me and I needed someone who knew which way to go. I did ***Lady on a Train*** with her. We were friends. I tested for the lead in ***Christmas Holiday*** and didn't get the part; it went to Gene Kelly. Deanna saw the test and said if I had done the part, the picture would have been better.

* * *

Q -I've seen a picture of you in your early career with a suit on and an ascot. You really look like a leading man. How did you get your cowboy break?

A - Universal was in the middle of changing hands with Eagle-Lion out of England at the time I had an option come up. They offered to keep me on at the same money, but I thought I'd go back to school and learn something. In the meantime, Bob Tansey did ***Song of Old Wyoming*** with Eddie Dean and Jennifer Holt, which started a new ballgame for me. I wound up doing that picture, which I have to give credit to for making me a drawing card for the rest of the Western films I made.

I don't know if you've heard the story of how I got cast in ***Song of Old Wyoming***, my first Western. Bob Tansey (the producer) had interviewed me for the part and told me to meet him later at his office. When I walked into his office, he was talking on the phone, so I waited until he got finished. Then he didn't speak to me; he called his secretary, Frances Kavanaugh*, and said to her, "Well, this is him. What do you think?" She just nodded her head.

Tansey said, "He looks the part if he can just act."

I said, "I'm probably the best actor that's every been in your office."

Tansey looked at his secretary and said, "Well, he's either good or he's nuts!" Then he looked back at me and said, "I had intended to use somebody who could use a whip."

I said, "A bullwhip?"

He nodded.

"I'm no expert," I quickly offered, "but I've been messing with one since I was a kid."

"Are you kidding me?" he asked.

"Why should I kid you?" What do you have to do with the whip?"

So he told me a couple of things he wanted done, and I asked how long a whip he thought I ought to have.

He said, "Eighteen or twenty feet."

I got the part, so I went out and rented two whips--one eighteen feet and one twenty. He told me I didn't have to be an expert, just make it believable that I could get it out in front of me. I beat myself to death trying to get that sucker out in front of me. I had welts on my back that never did go away! I had never had a whip in my hand before that time! (audience laughter)

So three days later (when Tansey had seen the film's first rushes) he said to me, "You're doing a great job, Al. How would you like to do three pictures at three times the money you're making for this one?"

I said, "That sounds good, Bob, but I'd better tell you something. I can't handle that whip."

His face dropped to his chest and he said, "But you said—"

I said, "Wait a minute now, you doubted if I could act, so I just acted. I acted as if I could use a whip!" (audience laughter) I pulled my shirt up and showed Bob the welts across my back and one up high on my neck where I'd really hurt myself with the whip. I told him the whole story, and he thought it was the funniest thing he had ever heard.

* * *

In this photo from the 1986 Charlotte Film Fair, Lash is seen with Eddie Dean, the star of the first Western in which he appeared. Next to Lash is Shirley Patterson, Eddie's leading lady in several films.

---

*Lash always referred to Frances Kavanaugh as Tansey's secretary when he told this story. In fact, she was the screenwriter on ***Song of Old Wyoming***.

Q -You obviously learned how to use the whip effectively. Who taught you?

A - Tansey hired a fellow by the name of Snowy Baker to teach me how to handle a whip. Before the picture was over, I could handle one. When the fan mail started coming in to the guy that used the whip, I figured there must be something there, so I learned how to handle the thing real good. I became the best. Every time I heard of somebody who did anything with a whip, I went to see him, no matter how far it was. I believe I was the best in the world. Not patting myself on the back, but I've had a lot of people try to copy me, and very few did. I'm very proud of the fact that Whip Wilson's series was put together because of the strength of my pictures.

* * *

Q -How long did it take to learn to open a Coke bottle with your whip?

A - That was an accident the first time. I was working out a new whip I had just gotten when one of the boys commented that he didn't have an opener for the Coke he wanted to drink. I said, "Hold it out and I'll take the cap off." He held it out and, sure enough, I took it off. It was an accident at the time. We perfected the trick later and put it in my act.

* * *

Q -Where can I get a whip like you use?

A - I wish I knew where to get some good whips today. I'd like to get a dozen of them myself. It's kind of a lost art; they aren't making good whips anymore. Some fair whips are coming out of Australia, but they are charging so much for them that it's ridiculous. I think Nudie in Hollywood wanted a hundred and something for a twelve-foot whip, and that's a little silly to me. I usually started out with a fifteen-foot whip, but each time I'd break it, I'd cut it down a little bit. I've got one now that started out as an eighteen-foot

The actors playing outlaws must have had a lot of faith in Lash's ability with the whip. They were almost certain to encounter it sometime in the film.

Lash LaRue was in attendance as *The Nashville Palace* honored Roy Rogers' 50th year in show business, aired on November 7, 1981. On stage, left to right: Jock O'Mahoney, Lash LaRue, George Montgomery, Montie Montana. In stage: Eddie Dean, Rex Allen, Sr. Standing: Monte Hale, Tex Williams, Iron Eyes Cody, Dale Evans, Roy Rogers, Linda (Hayes) Crosby, Pat Buttram, Sunset Carson. Front row: The Sons of the Pioneers (Doc Denning, Roy Lanham, Dale Warren, Rusty Richard, and Luther Nallie).

whip and now it's nine!

* * *

Q -When Roy Rogers celebrated his 50th year in show business several years ago, there was a special *Nashville Palace* television show with you and a whole passel of Western stars. Pat Buttram was the person introducing all of the guest stars. I remember when Pat introduced you, you cracked your whip and knocked Pat's hat off with the backlash from the whip. He had the most startled look on his face when that happened. I wondered what he said to you about that off camera.

A - The director cut Pat's line when that happened. Pat said, "Ouch, I'm glad I didn't work with him!" (audience laughter) Actually, you can't watch the backlash on a whip in close quarters like that, but I didn't hurt anybody. I just knocked his hat off. I can't blame him a bit for having a startled look on his face! (audience laughter)

* * *

Q -Did you ever hurt anybody with your

whip?

A - No, I didn't. I used to pull children out of the audience to work with me when I had my exhibition rodeo. They would hold a paper in their hands, and I would cut it just a little bit at a time. I was very proficient with the whip. The mothers would be scared to death, but the kids would just stand there like Trojans. I never hurt anybody.

* * *

Q - Do you still have the original black suit you wore in pictures?

A - This is it! (audience laughter) Bob Tansey let me go down to Western Costuming and pick out my own wardrobe for ***Song of Old Wyoming***. I wore a shirt that George O'Brien had used in one of his pictures. I kind of liked George O'Brien, anyway. I wore the shirt with the hope that some of him would rub off on me. I still wear black; I wore black before it got popular! (audience laughter) In fact, I got fan mail addressed to the guy who wore the black outfit. I also got fan mail addressed to the guy who used the whip—they didn't even know my name! And a funny thing was that I was especially popular with black audiences.

Lash is seen here at the 1984 Raleigh, North Carolina, Film Fair with Western fan Tom Wyatt and Charles "Durango Kid" Starrett.

Lash poses in a publicity still for *Dead Man's Gold.*

In a parade one time in California, the kids lining the street in a white section of town didn't show much recognition when I rode through. When I got to the black section of town, the kids yelled, "Hey, that's the Cheyenne kid!" They knew me right away.

* * *

Q - When you started your film career, did you want to become a cowboy star?

A - When I was a little boy, I used to pray to be a cowboy. Outside of my immediate family, the only ones I had respect for were the cowboys who did good things and then rode off into the sunset. I wanted to be a cowboy. My heroes on the screen were William S. Hart, Tom Mix, Hoot Gibson, and Ken Maynard.

* * *

Q - You just mentioned your family. How did they react when they saw you on the screen for the first time?

A - My mama went to see ***Song of Old Wyoming***, and I got killed in it. She sat there and cried like a baby. I tried to explain that I had not passed on, but still the tears came. I knew I was an actor; I had convinced her that I was gone! (audience laughter) I didn't let any of my family come out and see my pictures being made. I wouldn't let anybody visit me. I don't know what the reason was; I just didn't want my family there because I was doing a job and I didn't want them... I didn't want to explain what I was doing; maybe I didn't know what I was doing. (audience laughter)

* * *

Q - Do you consider that person on the screen yourself or somebody else?

A - No, it's me before I grew up. I was an adult adolescent for a long time.

* * *

Q - Was it really the huge amount of Lash LaRue fan mail that PRC Pictures received that caused you to get a contract for your own starring series?

A - A studio of that size pays attention to fan mail, especially when they get boxes of

Lash proves again that he's not one to be messed with. That's Jack Holt standing behind Lash in this scene from *The Daltons' Women.*

it. Here I was, a guy who came in from left field and, all of a sudden, people liked me in the pictures. I got some great fan mail from all over the world.

* * *

Q - Why did PRC Pictures have such low budgets?

A - I often wondered that myself! (audience laughter)

* * *

Q - Where were your pictures filmed?

A - We used the Monogram Ranch, Corriganville, and Iverson's Ranch for most of our locations. It was a lot of fun filming on location.

* * *

Q - How long did it take to make one of your PRC or Western Adventure productions films?

A - It usually took about five days. We didn't waste any time or money! (audience

This fellow looks as it he can tell Lash and Fuzzy exactly what's been happening in town.

laughter)

* * *

Q - Please comment on some of the people you worked with in your films.

A - I was so thrilled to work with people like Charley King; Bud Osborne; Jack Holt; his lovely daughter, Jennifer Holt; and another of my leading ladies, Peggy Stewart. They were all great. And there are a lot of other guys and ladies whose names I forget right this minute. I used to enjoy Charley, Bud, and Jack Holt in movies before I got into pictures myself. To have them on my show was just fantastic. Charley King was a wonderful person; everybody loved working with him. He usually played a heavy, but in ***Caravan Trail*** with Eddie Dean and me, he was a comic sidekick and great! I cried when I heard about his death. He died in the Actors' home; he had a broken back. If the actors hadn't gotten together and gotten him in, he wouldn't have had any place at all. I think it's a shame. If Charley King could have seen the love and admiration that we see from you fans today, it would have made him feel that it was all worthwhile.

Time passes so quickly. A boy came running up to me, must have been six-foot-four—like Sunset Carson—and said, "I've been seeing your pictures ever since I was a kid."

I said, "How old are you, boy?"

He said, "Nineteen!" (audience laughter)

The business has been wonderful to me. There is no other way in the world I could have learned what I learned and still been alive if I had done it any other way. I sure thank God for the experience to be around these people we have been talking about.

* * *

Q - How did you memorize all of those lines of dialogue for your films?

A - We didn't film the stories in sequence, so in order to know where I was from page three to thirty-eight, I had to know the story very well. I used to read it over many times and then spot study the dialogue for the scenes we were about to shoot. If I knew what was happening in the story from beginning to end, I knew the type of reaction I was supposed to have at any point in the script.

* * *

Q - Do you remember anybody who ever held up the shooting for a long time because of fluffing lines?

A - Yeah, I did. (audience laughter) One of my directors, Ray Taylor, never got mad. He was *so* calm. I remember in one picture I had a scene with four names and two different towns. I kept messing it up; I must have done it thirteen different times! We couldn't afford to do that. I got mad at him for not getting mad at me! (audience laughter)

* * *

Q - How does it feel working as an actor in front of cameras?

A - Being an actor is pretty easy. All you have to do is act natural when it's under an unnatural circumstance. (audience laughter) I enjoyed it, all of it—the stories, the people, the cameraman, and the crew—we had a lot of fun. We had a crew on those films that was simply amazing. We got more film in the can per dollar spent than anybody else in the business. Other companies used to send people over to try to figure out how we did it. It was because we all liked each other, and we all worked together—and that's important!

You fans made me a star when the motion picture people didn't want to mess with me. As I said before, it was your fan mail addressed to the guy who wore the black outfit—that's why I still wear black—

, or to the guy that used the whip, or the guy who played the part of the Cheyenne Kid in ***Song of Old Wyoming*** that got me my own starring series.

* * *

Q - How many times were you injured during the filming of your pictures?

A - I got my nose broken once, but that was my fault. I just didn't duck right during a fight scene. I hurt my back when my horse shied while I was doing a transfer. I didn't have footing, and I messed up my back. We were generally very careful. Back in the days before stunts became such a big business, we had prayer book stunt men. They were people with more guts than brains. Then along came Yakima Canutt, and he had a little program for putting some science into stunting. He developed a lot of the things they are using today. He was a great asset to the industry. Davey Sharpe was another stunt man who was just fantastic!

* * *

Q - Who was your favorite director?

A - I had a lot of good directors, but my favorite was my cameraman. We had a great cameraman! Ernie Miller was his name, and he was also a director for me. Because of the low budgets, if the director got a scene that could be seen and heard, he'd say, "Print it!" Ernie would sometimes say, "Just a minute. I think we can get one better for the camera." He would then tell me something that would improve the scene. He was a great guy!

* * *

Q - What is you favorite film, not necessarily your own?

A - I worked in a picture with Dick Powell and Linda Darnell years ago called ***It Happened Tomorrow***. I don't know, it didn't get played very much, but I enjoyed the story very much.

Here is an unusual picture. Lash LaRue and Jack Holt's double fight it out in a scene from *The Daltons' Women.*

* * *

Q - Which of your starring films do you like best?

A - I think probably the twin-brother film, ***Outlaw Country***, was my favorite. We created the Frontier Phantom character, Lash's brother, and I wound up playing both characters and working twice as hard for the same money. I had a lot of fun with it. If I had known a little bit more about the technical part, I would have talked to the sound man before I started, because I was playing it one way and he was playing it another—but it turned out all right. The producer stole scenes out of that one and made two pictures of it. They always find some way of messing things up. They used a lot of scenes from my pictures over and over again, and that always bugged me. It seemed to me if you were going to make two pictures, it ought to be two separate pictures. I liked doing the twin because it was a challenge to my ability to change the personality, and I think I did a pretty good job.

* * *

Q - Did you ever play a dual role in any other films?

A - I also did one for Russ Hayden in the TV series ***26 Men.*** I like to play dual roles; it's kind of a challenge for an actor. I always like to test myself out a little bit in my acting.

* * *

Q - Would you reminisce about the whip fight in ***King of the Bullwhip***?

A - I enjoyed making ***King of the Bullwhip***. If a major studio were doing the ending whip fight, they would have taken about two weeks. We did it in one afternoon. We were on a budget, so we *had* to do it in one afternoon. That's why they called them B Westerns; we never went over budget because the studio didn't have any more money! (audience laughter) Dennis Moore, who was supposed to be in the whip fight with me, couldn't handle one, so we brought in a double to do the whip fight. The fight looks great in the film, but it's no big deal to use a whip. If you can fly cast looking for a trout, you can learn to use a whip also. It's the same principle.

* * *

Q - What was the name of the horse you used in your Westerns?

A - Black Diamond. I tried to change it to Rush, but it didn't work. Black Diamond was out of quarter horse stock; he was great! I'd let him out to pasture while I was on the road. When I'd come back, I'd ride him out hard and walk back, talking to him on the way. I believe he understood me. I'd tell him about the dog food factories, and he would never mess up a scene. (audience laughter)

* * *

Q - When did you learn to ride?

A - I learned to ride when I was pretty young. I always loved horses, and when I was young I herded cattle. I wanted to be a cowboy, but I didn't associate herding cattle with being a cowboy. I always enjoyed riding. In fact, I still ride occasionally at a friend's place down in Georgia. I visit Georgia every once in a while; I have a couple of daughters down there.

* * *

Q - Didn't your producer, Bob Tansey, have some comments about your riding ability?

A - Bob Tansey was a very clever guy, and he was always coming up with a good quip. He was the one who said you should always be nice to the producer because tomorrow he might be the gate man and he wouldn't let you in the studio. I got a write-up on the picture ***Song of Old Wyoming*** in which he said, "He throws guns with the dash that great Western players have possessed since horse thrillers began. He rides as though glued to the saddle." Bob said, "It's the only way the son-of-a-bitch can stay on the horse!" (audience laughter)

* * *

Q - Did you have a choice on your sidekick or did the studio just choose Fuzzy for you?

A - They chose him, and I was fortunate that they picked Fuzzy. He and Buster Crabbe had been close friends on their series which immediately preceded mine. One day about six months after Fuzzy and I started working together, he walked up to me and said, "You know, I

Lash complemented his black outfit by riding a black quarter horse named Black Diamond in his Western film series.

wasn't going to like you, but you are all right!" From then on we became close friends. Fuzzy used to do comedy with Buster's swimming show during the summer months when they weren't working on pictures. That's why he didn't like me coming into the pictures and Buster leaving them.

Fuzzy was a good friend and a wonderful teacher. I learned a lot of things from him. He didn't know he was my teacher, but God put me with him so I could learn something. He was a pantomime artist back in the days when they didn't have sound. He taught me that thought photographs as well as sound. I enjoyed every minute I was with him; I miss him.

* * *

Q - He was very acrobatic, wasn't he?

A - He was fantastic! He was like a piece of spring steel. He used to think of Fuzzy as a separate character from himself. He would see something funny and say, "That would be cute for Fuzzy to do." That's a wonderful way to be able to separate yourself from your show career.

* * *

That's Charles King at the table with Lash and Fuzzy.

Lash and Fuzzy plan strategy with popular leading lady Peggy Stewart.

Q - Is it true that Fuzzy had a bad drinking problem?

A - Yes. I tried to get him off hooch; the bottle had him pretty bad. I couldn't understand why he wouldn't try to stop, because it was killing him. Then I met his wife and I understood. She would have driven anyone to drink! She was a hypochondriac who went all over the country looking for a doctor who wanted to operate. She found a few. She died ahead of Fuzzy and left all of his money to her son by a previous marriage. Fuzzy didn't have a very happy home life. In fact, he couldn't even sign his check from the studio. The check was made out to him *and* her. He had to sign it and give it to her. And that's the way it was all through his life, I think. She was more like a keeper to him than anything I ever saw. She was the boss.

* * *

Q - Did you keep in contact with Fuzzy during the last years of his life?

A - No. I lost contact with Fuzzy late in his life. After his first wife died, he thought he had to have somebody to tell him what to do, I guess, so he married again, and she kept him working until he died. I'm sorry I wasn't there when he passed through. He died between shows on a personal appearance. He was resting at a motel between shows when he had a heart attack and died. But that's an easy way to go, and I'm glad he didn't suffer.

* * *

Q - How was Fuzzy to work with?

A - He was a beautiful person and a lot of fun to work with. His important dialogue was generally shot in the morning because during lunch somebody would slip him a drink and he'd mumble. He could stumble over a match stick and spend fifteen exiting minutes looking for the match. I loved the man. I learned a lot of things working with him. He had been in the business since the silent days. He taught me a lot about acting that I couldn't have learned any other way. Of course, the bottle killed him. I wish I had known something then so that I could have helped him.

* * *

Q -How would Fuzzy react if he could see you in a beard today?

A - He'd say, "Lash, you have to shave that beard!" Fuzzy was an angel unaware. He didn't understand the whole story of the life and death monopoly of the soul, but he was a beautiful person. Fuzzy was just Fuzzy; you couldn't duplicate him if you tried. I don't really think of him as gone; the spirit of him will be here forever.

* * *

Q -What did you do after your film series ended?

A - For quite a few years I toured. I hit just about every part of the country on my tours. I was surprised when I was booked to play the New York State Fair at Syracuse. I didn't think I'd do very well, but I jammed and packed them in up there. I did a show one time and they had never seen a picture I'd made, but my comic books were very popular in that particular area. In eleven southern states

Lash LaRue and Fuzzy St. John disguised as holdup men.

my films were top Western draws at the box office, so my tours throughout the South were particularly popular. I'll never forget the time we were traveling in the South and a little boy came up to my producer and director, Ron Ormond, and me. The boy recognized me from my pictures and didn't know quite what to make of me. He said to Ron, "Is he real?"

Ron, looking over at me, said, "Yes, he's real."

The boy asked, "If'n I was to cut him, would he bleed?" (audience laughter) I'm sure glad he asked!

* * *

Q -I've heard that your comic book was one of the fastest selling during the early 1950s. Is that correct?

A - Roscoe Fawcett told me it was the fastest-rising comic book since *Superman.* That comic book of mine has always been amazing to me. They had a great crew, Fawcett did. I didn't care much for the operation at Charlton, the company that later did the comic book. Charlton was

The Lash LaRue comic books have become collector's items in recent years and have greatly increased in value. It's interesting and not a little puzzling what makes one comic sky-rocket in price while another, featuring an equally popular character, languishes.

kind of a schlock outfit, and they messed it up. The Fawcett publication was very high-class. They did a couple of my films in comic book form. They were very popular. I saw one today in the dealer's room—*Vanishing Outpost*.

I once advertised a whip on the back of some of my comic books. When we couldn't get production on the whip, I had to refund 600 dozen money orders. It cost me seventy-five cents apiece to send them back. That's sort of the story of my life! (audience laughter)

The comic books sold twelve million copies a year in four languages. I shared the *Six-Gun Hero* comic with Hopalong Cassidy, Rocky Lane—I forget who else was included. They had different ones they put in every so often, but they had me on the cover more than fifty percent of the time. It's amazing; they have become collector's items.

They made a comic book out of one of my feature pictures, which I was anxious to get. Some kid brought it up to me at a Western film festival to autograph. I thought maybe I could buy it from him and asked how much he paid for it. He said "Twenty dollars." It is a ten-cent comic book, of course. I said, "I'll give you thirty dollars for it." "Oh, I wouldn't sell I for anything," he told me. It's amazing how prices have jumped up for these types of things. You can't buy a three-sheet or a one-sheet, window cards or anything of mine anymore.

*   *   *

Q - Do you think that facially they reproduced you well in the comic book?

A - Oh, yeah. I think that Fawcett did a great job. Of course, they had me doing some things in the comics that just don't seem quite right. In one of them I was falling down a well and flipped the whip up and pulled myself out. Now, you can't do that! I can't do that! They had some good imagination, and the kids really loved them.

*   *   *

Q - Are the comics still being published?

A - No, not now, but there was a comic book company putting out a Lash LaRue comic around 1983. I called them and asked where the royalties were. They said, "We thought you were dead!"

*   *   *

Q - Didn't you have a television series for a while in North Carolina?

A - Yeah, I had a show that was on one station in Charlotte, North Carolina. I ramrodded the show for twenty-six weeks, and then they figured they had enough to run forever, so they quit paying me—but they were still showing the programs. We had an awful time getting those stopped. I think they're still showing them once in a while. Nothing serious, but at least they could send me a Christmas card once a year! (audience laughter)

*   *   *

Q - Weren't you on the "Wyatt Earp" television series during the 1960s with Hugh O'Brian?

A - How many of you remember the "Wyatt Earp" show? (audience applause) Yes, I was on the show for a year as the sheriff of Cochise County. Hugh O'Brian and I didn't get along too good. (laugh) I had heard from the fellow that furnished the horses on my exhibition rodeo that O'Brian had offered a thousand dollars to anyone who could beat him on the draw. My wrangler told me that it would be the softest thousand I ever made, because he had seen both of us work a draw. I told him that maybe O'Brian was faster than he figured, and besides, I didn't want to be part of O'Brian's publicity.

So here I was now in O'Brian's se-

Behind the boulder, with gun in hand, Lash is ready for the cameras to roll.

ries and we had a scene where he was supposed to beat me on the draw. We were set up so that both of us were in the scene on camera.

I said, "Hugh, I'll make a nervous gesture before I draw."

He said, "You don't have to cue me, Speedy. You can draw any time." (audience laughter)

That kind of hurt my feelings, and I thought I'd just check this sucker out. The first time he didn't get his gun out before I had mine on him.

The director yelled, "Cut! Slow it down, Lash."

We got all set up and went with the scene again. This time I had blanks in the gun, so I pulled and fired before he got his gun out!

The director shouted, "Damn it, Lash, can't you slow it down?"

I said, "No. I'd like to kill him!" (audience laughter)

* * *

Q - Didn't you star in a couple of science fiction films during the 1980s?

A - Yes, I made them in North Carolina. One is called ***The Dark Power*** and the other is ***Alien Outlaw***. ***The Dark Power*** was made up around Kernersville. ***Alien Outlaw*** was made up near Sparta. The Sparta Chamber of Commerce gave me a T-shirt. On the front it says, "Where is Sparta, North Carolina?" On the back it says, "Who the hell cares!" (audience laughter) The pictures have been released to foreign markets, and one is out on home video.

I don't know too much about the business part of it. If I had been a good

Lash is seen here on location in North Carolina for the filming of *The Dark Power.*

The
Neighborhood
is Going to Hell. . .
WELCOME TO
GREENSBORO
POPULATION:
NOW GO HOME
THE
DARK
POWER
NEW VISION PRODUCTIONS, LTD. and TRIAD MOTION PICTURES, INC.
present
THE DARK POWER
starring LASH LARUE • ANNA LANE TATUM • CYNTHIA BALLEY • MARY DALTON
written and directed by PHIL SMOOT produced by PHIL SMOOT and GEORGE B. WALKER
Now Available on Videocassette
MAGNUM
ENTERTAINMENT

ONLY ONE WOMAN
HAD THE GUTS
TO FIGHT BACK . . .
OUTLAW
A.L.I.E.N
TRIAD MOTION PICTURES, INC. PRESENTS
ALIEN OUTLAW
Starring LASH LA RUE • Introducing KARI ANDERSON
With PAUL HOLMAN, GIL NEWSOM, RICHARD DAVIS, LIZ WARRINGTON, DEBORAH BRADY
Special Appearances By SUNSET CARSON And WILD BILL CODY • Director of Photography PAUL HUGHEN
Music Composed By MARCUS KEARNS • Associate Producer JOHN G. WOLFE III
Produced By PHIL SMOOT And GEORGE B. WALKER • Written And Directed By PHIL SMOOT
© Copyright MCMLXXXVII

businessman, I'd own this hotel we're in! (audience laughter) If my residuals ever catch up with me, I'm going to buy a piece of Hollywood and burn it! (audience laughter)

* * *

Q - What are the plots of the two films?

A - Well, ***The Dark Power*** has kind of a weak story, but it has a lot of action. I didn't care much for it myself. I guess that's what they're buying now. I can't understand it; we had simple stories with a little moral back in the days of my Westerns. I like the old simple Western-type story.

* * *

Q - Could you tell us a little more about the plots?

A - Can't I get around that at all? (audience laughter) The politicians do pretty well at avoiding answers! (audience laughter) ***Alien Outlaw*** is a story about another planet where they have a sport of killing people. Sunset Carson has a part in ***Alien Outlaw***. We were proud to have him with us.

* * *

Q - Weren't you in a picture with Johnny Cash not too long ago?

A - I did one that I'm real proud to be in—not much of a part, but I was in ***Stagecoach*** with Johnny Cash, Waylon Jennings, and Willie Nelson. I went over to visit them,

Lash, *Colt-45* star Wayde Preston, author David Rothel, and director/writer Oliver Drake are seen here at the 1986 Charlotte Western Film Fair during the guest star panel session.

and I wound up in their picture. I was just in it for a second. My one line was, "Well, the way I look at it, Luke, it's not my fight—yet!" That was my career. (audience laughter)

They're wonderful people. I know Waylon was a fan of mine when he was a little boy. He tells the story about seeing me (when he was a youngster) that has made national press and coverage on national television. I wanted to meet him. I had never met Johnny Cash in person. I was thrilled to meet them, and Johnny Cash said, "Lash, I've met a lot of important people, and I've never been nervous meeting anybody but you." I think the world is better off for having a Johnny Cash, Waylon Jennings, and a Willie Nelson.

You know, I was wearing black long before Johnny Cash. In Memphis a while back I was signing an autograph for his daughter, but I didn't know who she was. The fellow who was with me talked to her and found out who she was. When I finished signing, I handed it to her and she left.

He said, "Do you know who that was?"

I said, "No."

He said, "That's Rosanne, Johnny Cash's daughter."

I said, "Why didn't you say something so I could have spent some time with her? What did you say to her?"

He said, "I told her you were the *original* man in black."

I said, "That was a hell of a way to start! What did she say?"

"She said, 'We know.'" (audience laughter)

Johnny Cash was a fan of mine, and that's one reason why he decided to wear black. Johnny Cash, Waylon, Willie Nelson, and I were going to lunch together one day while they were making ***Stagecoach***. Waylon and I were walking in front, and Johnny and Willie were walking behind us. Johnny Cash said, "Look at me; I'm walking in my hero's footsteps." (audience laughter) They want me in their next picture. I hope I'm at my phone when they call.

* * *

Q - I understand that the Cash-Jennings-Nelson ***Stagecoach*** has some singing in it. Did you sing?

A - No, and you can be thankful for that! (audience laughter) Waylon and Johnny Cash did make a new album called *Heroes*, which has my picture and "Everlasting Peace" poem on the back. They've got their backs to the camera, and I have my whip down between them. It's a pretty album, nice picture. I've already got a lot of fan mail on it. (A lady hands Lash a copy of the album to show the audience.) This is the *Heroes* album; they dedicated it to me. I appreciate it a lot.

* * *

Q - The picture on the album makes it look as if you are taking the whip to Johnny and Waylon.

A - Yeah. Well they held still! I always get their attention when I've got that whip in my hand.

* * *

Q - I heard that you were in a music video with Johnny Cash and Waylon Jennings. Is that true?

A - Not that I know of. They might have used some excerpts from one of my pictures. Everybody uses a little of Lash LaRue, here and there. Nobody's sent me any money! (audience laughter)

* * *

Q - I'm very favorably impressed with your poetry. Are any of them available in print?

A - No, only the one on the *Heroes* album is in print. I've got them all up here in my

Here is a photograph which appeared on the Johnny Cash and Waylon Jennings "Heroes" record album cover, with a special dedication to the original man in black, Lash LaRue. This photograph was taken at the location of the TV movie *Stagecoach,* starring Johnny Cash, Waylon Jennings, and Kris Kristofferson.

head. If you don't like the way I say them, you won't like them at all. (audience laughter) I'm kidding. They're written down and I have tapes on the majority of them. Sometimes I just enjoy writing things out. As I say, none of them are published as of now. I guess after I get out of here some of them will be valuable. Robert Service never made any money until he was gone, you know. The same spirit that was with him, I think, is with me. I think God wrote it through Robert Service, and I think God writes it through me also.

*   *   *

Q - Have you considered recording some of the poems that you have written?

A - Yes, I have. I'm thinking seriously about recording them with some music background.

*   *   *

Q - What have you been up to lately?

A - Well, I do a little writing, and I'm trying to get back into the picture business in other type parts. I can't be what I was, and I'm trying to put the whip down. When I did the *David Letterman Show* on NBC television, I tried to get him to let me do some talking, but I ended up popping the whip again. As soon as I can put the whip down and start talking, I think I'll be able to do something character-wise. I'm working on it anyhow. Someone on television asked me what the name of my last picture was, and I said I haven't made it yet. (audience laughter)
I've been rehearsing forty years for one speech and nobody wants to hear it yet. I gave my heart to the Lord in 1963, and I stumbled around in the dark hallway of despair for a long time, but I think I know where I'm going and I'm going to try to get there as fast as I can.

*   *   *

Q -Do you have any regrets in your life?

A - I don't know where to start! (audience laughter) I had a certain amount of success that was just thrown at me. Success and money are two difficult things to handle, especially when you are a youngster. I guess it took me a few years to grow up. I appreciate the patience that everybody had who was associated with me.

*   *   *

Lash is seen here reciting one of his poems during a guest star panel session at the 1983 Charlotte Western Film Fair. Others on the panel are leading lady Jean Carmen, and Western star Fred Scott. Author David Rothel is the host.

Chapter 3
The Western Adventures of Lash LaRue
by Chuck Thornton

Song of Old Wyoming .... Cinecolor
65 Mins 1945

Eddie Dean .... Eddie
Al LaRue .... The Cheyenne Kid
Emmett Lynn .... Ezra
Jennifer Holt .... Vicky
Sarah Padden .... Ma Conway
John Carpenter .... Ranch hand
Ian Keith .... Lee Landow
Robert Barron .... Jessie Dixon
Lee Bennett .... Waco
Steve Clark .... Banker
Rocky Camron .... Ringo
Horace Murphy. .... Paper editor

Producer/Director Robert Emmett (Tansey)
Screenplay .... Frances Kavanaugh

Eddie Dean helps out his woman boss, Ma Conway (Sarah Padden), when rustlers and cattle barons try to break her. She also runs a newspaper which speaks out against the outlaws in the territory. When things aren't moving fast enough for the bad guys, Lee Landow and Jessie Dixon, they send the infamous Cheyenne Kid to speed things up. After the Cheyenne Kid successfully gets a job on Ma's ranch, he secretly starts to carry out his plans. He first rustles her cattle. After this, he blows up her watering hole, doing away with watering provisions. By this time, Eddie has started to suspect Cheyenne's hand in the goings on. There is also some jealousy from Eddie as Cheyenne starts to flirt with his girl, Vicky (Jennifer Holt).

As Eddie and a ranchhand named Ezra (Emmett Lynn) talk over the bad luck Ma has been having, especially since The Cheyenne Kid has arrived, Eddie notices that Ezra is carving a small Indian head out of wood with a very attractive knife. Ezra tells Eddie there is only one other knife like the one he has, that he gave the other one to Ma's son at a very early age and taught him to carve with it. He explains that the boy disappeared while still a child and has never been found.

Back in town, Cheyenne goes to Landow and Dixon, his outlaw bosses, and tells them that his job has been completed; Ma no longer has any cattle. He asks for his pay so that he can depart. Cheyenne is told that his job is not finished and that Ma has a newspaper office that she could fall back on even though she is almost bankrupt. He is told that after he blows up her newspaper, he will be paid in full. That night Cheyenne lays a few sticks of dynamite under her newspaper office and blows up the building.

Back in the bunkhouse, Eddie tells Cheyenne to stay away from Vicky because of his bad reputation. After Cheyenne calls her a cheap flirt, a fight breaks out between the two of them. Hearing the noise coming from the bunkhouse, Ma stops the fight with a shot from her shotgun.

After Cheyenne leaves for town, Eddie finds a knife on his bed, a knife just like the one Ezra has. Eddie also finds an Indian head carving similar to Ezra's. It is clear to Eddie that Cheyenne is Ma's long lost son.

When Cheyenne hears the story from Eddie, he becomes convinced that he really must be Ma's son. He confesses to Eddie that he is in the pay of Landow and Dixon and tells Eddie that he is going to Landow's place to get back all of the money so that Ma can replace her business.

When Cheyenne enters Landow's of-

fice, he is trapped by Landow's partner and has his guns taken away from him. He is ordered to leave. Cheyenne gets his bullwhip from his horse's saddle and then disarms one of Landow's men with the whip. Eddie and his men now arrive in town and start to have a gun battle with the outlaws. Now, with guns, Cheyenne has a showdown with Landow and Dixon. After being shot several times, Cheyenne stands long enough to get both of them.

Before Cheyenne dies in Eddie's arms, he tells Eddie never to tell Ma that he is her son. With Landow and Dixon now dead, Cheyenne has given his life to make things right for Ma Conway.

*   *   *

The Caravan Trail .... Cinecolor
57 Mins 1946

Eddie Dean .... Eddie
Lash LaRue .... Cherokee
Emmett Lynn .... Ezra
Jean Carlin .... Paula
Charles King .... Reno
Jack O'Shea .... Killer
Robert Malcolm .... Jim Bristol
Terry Frost. .... Barton
Forrest Taylor .... Judge
Robert Barron .... Joe King
Bob Duncan .... Poker Face

Producer/Director Robert Emmett (Tansey)
Screenplay .... Frances Kavanaugh

The story opens as Eddie Dean is leading a wagon train of settlers to their planned homesteads. Upon taking a break to set up camp for the night, they experience an attempted robbery by a dashing outlaw in black called The Cherokee Kid and his two pals Reno and Killer.

As Eddie gets the drop on Cherokee,he recognizes him as an old acquaintance that he thought had gone straight. Eddie orders Cherokee and his men to leave the camp, but the next day while on the trail again, Eddie drops a package of food purposely from a wagon for Cherokee and his men.

After the wagon train arrives in Red Rock, Jim Bristol, the head of the team, is killed after getting into an argument with Joe King, crooked owner of the saloon and land baron. King was supposed to have a piece of land for each of the settlers but has reneged on the deal after their arrival. When Dean becomes the new marshal, he arrests Poker Face, the man who shot Bristol, but not before having a fight with Joe King. Later, as shots are heard from the bank, Eddie once again runs into Cherokee, Killer, and Reno as they are attempting to rob the bank. Upon arresting them, Eddie gets an idea to fight fire with fire. He deputizes Cherokee and his pals in order to even up the fight against Joe King and his henchmen. On their first move, they break into King's safe and take the land deeds he has stolen. While Killer is keeping an eye on King's saloon, he is offered a better deal from King if he will turn on Dean and Cherokee by releasing Poker Face from jail. After Killer lets him out, Poker Face hits him across the head with his gun, killing him. Eddie trails Poker Face to his hideout where, after a battle, he lays Poker Face to the floor. King sends for a hired killer named Barton, Cherokee's most bitter enemy.

When Barton and his gang arrive in town, Eddie takes away Cherokee's guns so that he won't get into trouble with Barton. When Cherokee goes after Barton unarmed, Eddie realizes that he has made a mistake and throws Cherokee a rifle to shoot it out with Barton. After Eddie, Ezra, and Reno take care of Barton's henchmen, the town once again has peace restored. The wagon train gets on the trail again and Cherokee and Reno say their goodbyes to Eddie and Ezra as their trails lead to other adventures.

* * *

Wild West .... Cinecolor
75 Mins 1946
Eddie Dean .... Eddie
Lash LaRue .... Stormy Day
Roscoe Ates .... Soapy Jones
Sarah Padden .... Carrie Bannister
Robert "Buzz" Henry .... Skinny Bannister
Louise Currie .... Florabelle
Jean Carlin .... Mollie
Terry Frost .... Dawson
Lee Bennett .... Butler
Lee Roberts .... Captain Rogers
Chief Yowlachie .... Chief Black Fox
Bud Osborne, Bob Duncan,
Frank Pharr, Al Ferguson,
John Bridges .... Outlaws

Producer/Director......Robert Emmett (Tansey)
Screenplay.................Frances Kavanaugh

With outlaws stirring up the Indians and turning them against the building of the telegraph lines, three of the Rangers' best men are sent for—Eddie Dean, Stormy Day, and Soapy Jones. Upon their arrival, the Captain introduces them to Butler, the head man in charge of stringing the telegraph wire. Butler can't believe that only three men were sent to help him.

Eddie and the boys set up headquarters at the Bannister ranch. Carrie Bannister is the widow of Jim Bannister, a friend of the Rangers who was murdered by an unknown assailant. Carrie has a good relationship with the Indians. She sends her son, Skinny, after the Chief so that Eddie and Stormy may have a talk with him. They persuade the Chief to not interfere with the stringing of the wire and convince him to be patient so that they can prove that the tel-

egraph will help them to prosper as well as the white man.

Later, Eddie gets a hunch that the outlaws might try to destroy their supply cabin. Their equipment is removed only minutes before the outlaws blow up the cabin.

They set up a relay station in the stables hoping this time it will be unsuspected by the outlaws. However, upon returning from town, Butler and Soapy come upon a couple of varmints wrecking their equipment. Upon returning, Stormy hears the fighting going on inside and decides to join in on the excitement. With trusty bullwhip in hand, Stormy disarms one bad man while wrapping it around the neck of another.

With the culprits bested, Stormy and the boys take them to town for lock up. Later, the boys find out that the men they arrested have been released from jail by the judge and Dawson, a man who practically runs the town and also controls the crooked judge.

While on their way to deliver some money, Soapy and Skinny are chased by the outlaw gang. As Soapy eludes the gang, Skinny is shot from the saddle. While making sure who they shot, the head outlaw loses his gun. After the gang leaves, Soapy finds the gun and takes Skinny back to the ranch for doctoring.

Upon inspecting the gun, Eddie and Stormy find that it once belonged to their murdered friend, Jim Bannister. They know if they can find the man who has the mate to the gun, they will have their murderer.

Eddie and the boys ride hard to town, ready for a showdown. As they enter town, they notice that Dawson has his men staked out all over town. They enter their telegraph office only to be driven out by flaming torches thrown through the windows by Dawson's gang. A shootout breaks loose as the town goes wild.

With Soapy and Butler throwing sticks of dynamite at the henchmen in order to keep them back until the Cavalry arrives, Stormy gets into a fist fight with Dawson after learning that he has the mate to Bannister's gun.

One of Dawson's men jumps Eddie as

another one tries to sneak up the saloon stairs. Stormy manages to catch him around the neck with his bullwhip. After nearly tearing the saloon apart during the fight, Eddie and Stormy best their foes.

Now that Dawson and his men are cleaned up and the way has been made safe for the development of the telegraph, it is time for the boys to return to their headquarters.

Wild West was re-released in 1948 under the title ***Prairie Outlaws***. The re-release was in black and white instead of Cinecolor and was edited by fifteen minutes.

* * *

Law of the Lash

53 Mins .... February 28, 1947

Lash LaRue .... Cheyenne Davis
Fuzzy St. John .... Fuzzy Q. Jones
Lee Roberts .... Lefty
Mary Scott. .... Jane Hilton
Jack O'Shea. .... Decker
Charles King. .... Sheriff Rand
Carl Mathews. .... Blackie
Matty Roubert. .... Player
John Elliott. .... Pop Hilton
Charles Whitaker. .... .Bart
Ted French .... Player
Richard Cramer .... Bartender

Director .... Ray Taylor
Producer .... Terry Thomas
Screenplay .... William L. Nolte

Prospector Cheyenne Davis happens upon a recently held up stage while going to get supplies. After being told the details of the holdup he informs the driver that he will let the sheriff know what has happened.

Cheyenne arrives at the General Store and gets into trouble with an outlaw named Lefty who happens to have been on the stage robbery. Lefty is bullying Jane Hilton about supplies but Cheyenne bests him in a fight and persuades him to pay for the supplies he tried to take. He tries to pay with jewelry taken from a stage passenger but fails.

Cheyenne returns to his cabin and discusses with his partner, Fuzzy Q. Jones, how nice it would be to bag the reward money from the holdup, when Sheriff of Hagerstown arrives and congratulates him on how he handled himself at the store in Temecula. He talks Cheyenne and Fuzzy into looking into the town's lawlessness since it is out of his jurisdiction.

Lefty decides to track Cheyenne down, since he saw the stolen rings and follows Pop Hilton who is on his way to take supplies to the black-clad man.

Cheyenne is fired upon by Lefty as he and Hilton unload supplies. The outlaw is chased down and disarmed, and held at the cabin by Cheyenne.

Decker, leader of the outlaw gang in the area, is dismayed at the return of many townsfolk who had left town. He attributes their return to Cheyenne.

After having been held for three days by Cheyenne and Fuzzy without a single word being spoken Lefty is let go to walk back to town. About to have a breakdown because of all the silence, Lefty is most happy to leave.

On the long walk back, Lefty hears voices telling him what to do. As a result, he throws away the rings he had stolen in the stage holdup. Cheyenne, who is riding not far behind, returns the rings to a disturbed Lefty who believed he had seen the last of them.

Lefty finally arrives in Temecula and settles down for a drink only to have Decker come in and question him on the location of Cheyenne's shack. Decker sends his men to pay Cheyenne a visit, but they find no one

Fuzzy St. John uses his tongue as a telegraph receiver as Lash LaRue looks on in a scene from *Law of the Lash.*

there and return to town.

Cheyenne and Fuzzy watch Decker and his men from the Hilton's store and head for the saloon for a showdown. Cheyenne uses his whip and six-gun to battle his adversaries successfully. Realizing that Cheyenne is a marshal with whom he has had trouble before, Decker takes flight.

Cheyenne catches the outlaw leader and an exchange of gunfire occurs. The dapper Decker is unable to gun down Cheyenne who eventually whips the gun from his hand and escorts him to jail.

Now that law and order has been restored to the little town of Temecula, Cheyenne is free to leave. However, he has taken a liking to Jane and decides to stay.

* * *

Border Feud
55 Mins....May 10, 1947

Lash LaRue .... Cheyenne Davis
Fuzzy St. John .... Fuzzy Q. Jones
Ian Keith .... Dr. Peters
Gloria Marlen .... Carol Condon
Kenneth Ferrill .... Bob Hart
Ed Cassidy .... Sheriff
Bob Duncan .... Jack Barton
Casey Macgregor .... Jed Young
Brad Slavin .... Jim Condon
Mikel Conrad .... Elmore

Director .... Ray Taylor
Producer .... Jerry Thomas
Screenplay .... Patricia Harper
Story .... Joseph O'Donnell

U.S. Marshal Cheyenne Davis gets a let-

Lash LaRue and Fuzzy St. John are ready for action after yet another shooting in PRC's *Border Feud.*

ter from his friend Fuzzy Q. Jones, the sheriff of Red Gulch, Nevada, asking that he come assist him with the feud between the Hart and Condon families. Before leaving he is given a letter by the Mesa City sheriff that was taken from an outlaw just jailed who is known as the Tiger. The letter is signed with the letter E and requests that the Tiger come to Red Gulch to fuel the feud. Cheyenne retains the letter for future use.

In Jack Barton's Gold Nuggett Saloon, Fuzzy is posting a sign asking that all Harts and Condons check any guns with him when in public as a fight breaks out between Jim Condon and Bob Hart, owners of the Blue Girl Mining Co. Cheyenne arrives in time to whip the gun from a saloon patron about to shoot Jim.

Having knowledge that Barton is involved in summoning the Tiger to Red Gulch, Cheyenne enters Barton's office and finds the way clear to masquerade as the Tiger. Cheyenne is told by Barton that the Blue Girl Mine is worth over a million dollars and admits to having sent for the Tiger to help acquire it.

Retaining his marshal's badge, Cheyenne goes to see Dr. Peters, the town's most influential citizen, and introduces himself as the new marshal. Peters offers aid in any way possible, claiming to know the Harts and Condons quite well. Cheyenne meets Jim and his sister Carol at Peters' office and promises to help end the feud.

Cheyenne rides out to the Hart ranch but is stopped by an armed guard when he arrives. Cheyenne whips the rifle from his hand and beats him in a brief skirmish. He learns from the guard that Bob has gotten some men and headed for the Condon ranch for a confrontation.

Cheyenne gets Fuzzy and heads to

stop the showdown, but they arrive to the sound of gunfire. Jim and Bob are escorted to jail.

Later, as Barton and Cheyenne talk, Elmore, the man known as E, comes in and reveals to Barton that Cheyenne is not the Tiger. After Cheyenne admits to being an impostor, Barton tries to convince townsfolk that he is a criminal masquerading as a marshal so that he will be hung. Fuzzy arrives to help his friend escape.

Carol is kidnapped by Barton's men, and a note sent to Jim claims that she will be safe if he signs his share of the mine over to Bob. Jim shows the note to Cheyenne who feels it is a ruse, since Bob seems to be smitten with Carol. Cheyenne has Fuzzy dress as a woman and has Jim take him to Peters' office, hoping the crooks will believe he is Carol and go to where she is hidden to see what has happened.

The plan works and Cheyenne saves Carol. Fuzzy and Jim arrive to help rout the bandits but more of Barton's men arrive, indicating to Cheyenne that Peters is behind the trickery.

Cheyenne confronts Peters who gets away in a buckboard. He is caught and

Lash and Fuzzy keep their eyes on the outlaws before meting out some *Pioneer Justice.*

jailed, and the feud ends.

* * *

Pioneer Justice

56 Mins .... June 28, 1947
Lash LaRue .... Cheyenne Davis
Fuzzy St. John .... Fuzzy Q. Jones
Jennifer Holt .... Betty Walters
William Fawcett. .... Uncle Bob
Jack Ingram .... Bill Judd
Dee Cooper .... Criler
Lane Bradford.. Joe
Henry Hall .... Sheriff Peters
Steve Drake .... Al Walters
Bob Woodward .... Jackson
Terry Frost .... Grayson

Director .... Ray Taylor
Producer .... Jerry Thomas
Asst. Director............................... Ira Webb
Screenplay..............................Adrian Page

Cheyenne Davis and Fuzzy Q. Jones arrive in Buffalo Gap after finding the body of Deputy Jackson, whom they were to meet on the road. At the saloon they arrive to find more trouble as outlaw Bill Judd, who killed Jackson, has killed young Al Walters and is arguing with his sister Betty. Cheyenne whips a gun from Judd's hand and bests him in a free-for-all. The sheriff arrives but refuses to jail Judd.

Judd goes to a deserted shack and tells his boss, identified only by voice, of Betty's threat to get help from the marshal's office and the intervention of Cheyenne, who just happens to be a marshal. Judd is ordered

to get rid of both Betty and Cheyenne.

Betty informs Cheyenne that Judd has run off many of the ranchers but advises that she will stay. Uncle Bob, a rancher wiped out earlier by drought, promises to help her, as do Cheyenne and Fuzzy.

The next day Cheyenne and Fuzzy catch Judd and his men as they try to burn down Betty's ranch. After a fight, the men are held until night, at which time they are taken to jail. Sheriff Peters does not want to jail them, but Cheyenne forces him.

The next morning the outlaws are freed but are trailed to a deserted shack by Cheyenne and Fuzzy. The outlaws are chastised by their boss and are ordered to get rid of the area ranchers.

After leaving the shack hastily because of Fuzzy's sneeze, Cheyenne and his partner encounter Uncle Bob on the trail. They tell him to go look after Betty while they search the shack for clues.

After only finding spur marks on the shack table as clues, Cheyenne and Fuzzy meet Betty who tells them she believes Grayson (Terry Frost), the new town gambler, is involved in some way. After Fuzzy engages him in a card game and gets into trouble, Cheyenne hauls Grayson off to Betty's ranch for questioning. He is about to name his boss when he is shot.

Uncle Bob rides up and claims to have been kidnapped by the outlaws. He takes Cheyenne, Fuzzy, and Betty to the shack Cheyenne came upon before. Once inside, Cheyenne accuses Uncle Bob of being the outlaw boss. Uncle Bob pulls a gun and admits to wanting all property in the area because he was first to settle in Buffalo Gap.

Fuzzy shoots the gun from his hand, but before they are able to leave, Judd and his men and the sheriff arrive and pepper the shack with hot lead. Caught like rats, Cheyenne stops shooting to hopefully draw the outlaws in. The trap works and all are captured except Judd who is able to flee on foot until he is run down by Cheyenne, who kills him in a shootout.

With Uncle Bob and the rest of his law-

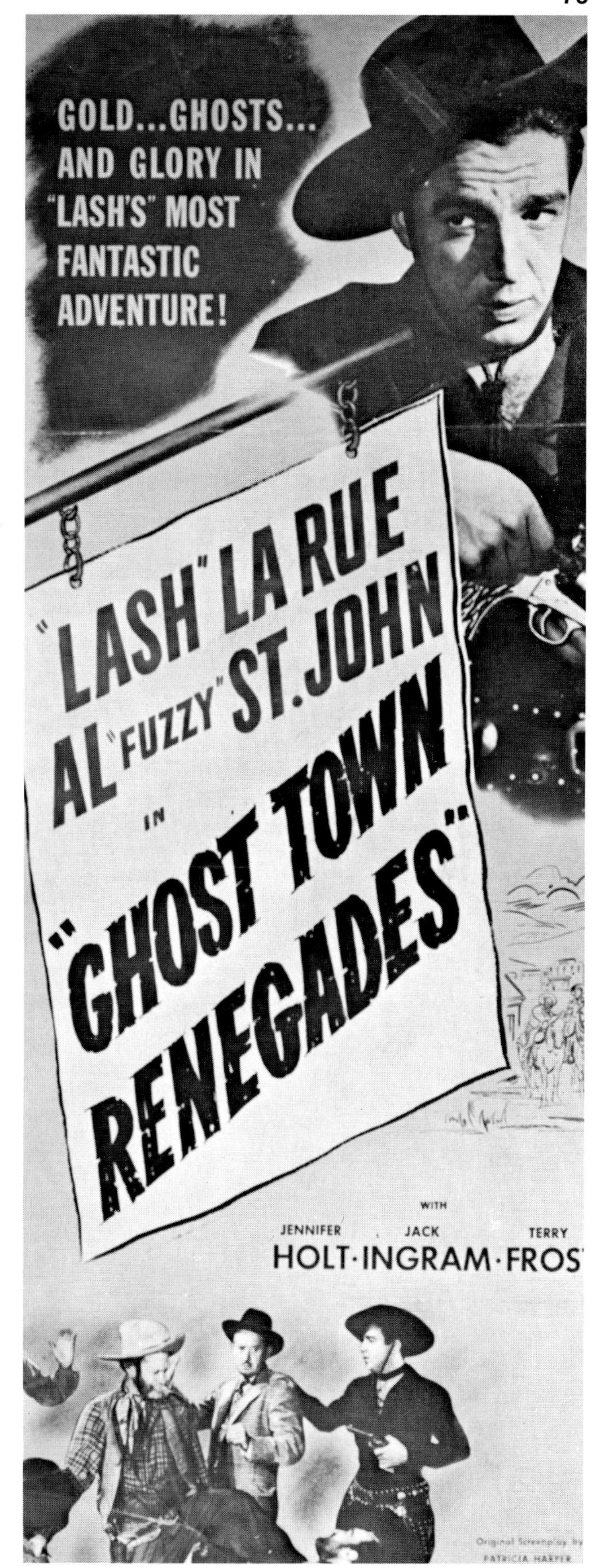

less faction now no longer a danger to Betty Walters and the peaceful citizens of Buffalo Gap, the man in black prepares to move on for adventures elsewhere, leaving Fuzzy behind to serve as the new sheriff.

* * *

Ghost Town Renegades

57 Mins .... July 26, 1947

Lash LaRue .... Cheyenne Davis
Fuzzy St. John .... Fuzzy Q. Jones
Jennifer Holt .... Diane Trent
Jack Ingram .... Vance Sharpe
Terry Frost .... Flint
Steve Clark .... Rodney Trent
Lee Roberts .... Johnson
Lane Bradford...................................... Waco
Henry Hall .... Marshall Jennings
William Fawcett .... Jonas Watson
Dee Cooper .... Player
Mason Wynn...................................... Player

Director .... Ray Taylor
Producer .... Jerry Thomas
Screenplay........................... Patricia Harper

Cheyenne Davis is dispatched by Marshal Jennings to Waterhole to locate a missing federal surveyor. He is glad to hear he will join Fuzzy Q. Jones, his partner, who is there masquerading as a prospector.

On the way, Cheyenne saves Rodney Trent, a Waterhole heir, after he has been wounded by outlaws Flint and Waco. Fuzzy arrives, and he and his partner take Trent to a deserted shack for treatment. Cheyenne learns that Trent answered an ad asking all Waterhole heirs to come to Barton City to see Vance Sharpe. Cheyenne and Fuzzy leave Trent to recover as they ride to see that his daughter, Diane, who is also enroute, does not meet a similar fate.

Lash LaRue returns Jennifer Holt's will to prove he is not a crook in PRC's *Ghost Town Renegades.*

Fuzzy St. John, Jennifer Holt, and Lash LaRue are held at bay by outlaw boss Jack Ingram and his henchmen Terry Frost and Lane Bradford in *Ghost Town Renegades.*

Flint and Waco try to waylay the stage in which Diane is a passenger, but Cheyenne sees them, cuts across country, and takes her off the stage after her driver is shot. When in a safe place, she is told of the attack on her father. The brave lass suggests that she be used as bait to apprehend those behind the attacks.

Cheyenne and Diane go to Sharpe's office and have him draw up a will for her with Cheyenne named executor in order to protect her and force the crooks to try to get Cheyenne too.

Cheyenne tells Trent that Diane is safe and updates him on what has been done. Waco spots Cheyenne and Trent at the deserted shack and tells Sharpe, who is behind the attacks since he knows of a new gold vein at Waterhole.

Sharpe tries to discredit the man in black and his partner and tells Diane they are crooks holding her father captive. Unfortunately, Diane believes him, especially when she overhears Cheyenne tell Sharpe, in an effort to trick him, that he is also out to gain the valuable land.

Cheyenne and Fuzzy find Trent dead at the shack. Sharpe, Diane, Flint, and Waco arrive and accuse the lawmen of murder. A fight takes place, but Cheyenne and Fuzzy come out on top and ride off with Diane.

At Waterhole Cheyenne returns the will to Diane to convince her of his innocence. Upon learning that Sharpe told her where her father was, Cheyenne and Fuzzy return to search his office. They find a letter indicating that Johnson, also a Waterhole heir, will arrive tomorrow.

Cheyenne intercepts and briefs Johnson and pretends to kill him. The outlaws arrive and haul the man off but are followed by Cheyenne and Fuzzy. Johnson is about to be buried, but the lawmen enter, engage them in a brawl, and find the remains of the federal surveyor.

Sharpe shoots and kills assayer Jonas Watson who has helped him to forge land deeds and is about to flee when Cheyenne arrives. Sharpe gets away but is caught and soundly thrashed by Cheyenne.

Before leaving, Cheyenne learns of the new gold vein in Waterhole and that it's discovery will again bring prosperity to the former ghost town.

* * *

Return of the Lash

61 Mins .... Oct. 11, 1947
Lash LaRue .... Cheyenne Davis
Fuzzy St. John .... Fuzzy Q. Jones
Mary Maynard .... Kay Grant
Brad Slaven .... Tom Grant
George Chesebro .... Big Jim Kirby
Lee Morgan .... Dan Clark
Lane Bradford .... Dave
John Gibson .... Pete
Dee Cooper. .... Player
Roy Butler .... Sheriff
George Denormand .... Jeff Harper
Carl Matthews .... Outlaw
Charles Whitaker .... Outlaw

Director .... Ray Taylor
Producer .... Jerry Thomas
Asst. Director .... Ira Webb
Screenplay .... Joseph O'Donnell

Sage Brush merchant Big Jim Kirby, seeking to gain control of all land in the area since he knows that the railroad is coming through, causes much trouble in his quest for same. Jeff Harper is also fighting for control. The resulting feud causes much trouble and lawlessness for the town, so Tom Grant sends for Cheyenne Davis to help out. His partner Fuzzy Q. Jones is already in town, sent on earlier to size up the situation.

Cheyenne is enroute to Sage Brush when Dave and two other Kirby henchmen try to prevent his arrival. The man in black shoots one and disarms another using his whip.

Cheyenne makes it to the Grant ranch and is talking over the town's problems with Tom, his sister Kay, and partner Fuzzy when Dan Clark arrives, having been chased there by Kirby, Dave, and Pete. Kirby and his men arrive prompting a donnybrook. After being roughed up, Kirby warns Tom to sell out before the trouble escalates.

Tom's friend, Harper, comes in and is introduced to Cheyenne, who is made aware that Harper has bought up a number of ranches and wants to buy Tom's to control water rights.

Cheyenne and Fuzzy learn from the sheriff that Kirby's gunmen are wanted men with a total reward of $33,000 payable if captured. They round up the outlaws and decide to use the money to prevent foreclosure on the ranches. Clark persuades Harper to advance the money until the actual reward money comes from Kingston.

Fuzzy is sent to get the money. He is on his way back when Dave and Pete prepare to jump him. Fuzzy is able to hide the money but is beaten up, causing him to lose

Lash LaRue collars George Chesebro as sheriff Roy Butler guards Lane Bradford in *Return of the Lash.*

his memory of where he hid the money.

Having just thirty days to deliver the ranchers' deeds to the railroad, Kirby plans to acquire the Grant ranch so he can control the water rights and force others to sell.

Fuzzy comes to and remembers where he hid the money. With Kirby and his men now jailed, the citizens of Sage Brush can return to a peaceful life.

* * *

The Fighting Vigilantes

61 Mins .... October 22, 1947
Lash LaRue .... Cheyenne Davis
Fuzzy St. John .... Fuzzy Q. Jones
Jennifer Holt............................Abby Jackson
George Chesebro.....................Price Taylor
Lee Morgan .... Sheriff
Marshall Reed ....Check
Carl Matthews.....................................Shanks
Russell Arms.......................................Player
Steve Lark.............................Frank Johnson
John Elliott .... Bert
Felice Richmond .... Ellie

Director .... Ray Taylor
Producer .... Jerry Thomas
Asst. Director................................ Ira Webb
Screenplay...................Robert B. Churchill

While standing in the road, Fuzzy Q. Jones is almost run down by Abby Jackson, so he and Cheyenne Davis go after the young lady. Before catching her, three masked gunmen overtake her and ransack her buckboard. The gunmen are run off by Cheyenne and Fuzzy who then escort Abby home.

Cheyenne and Fuzzy go to town after leaving Abby and immediately run into the bandits—Check, Shanks, and a third man. After questioning and subduing them, they take them to jail.

As the sheriff locks the men up, merchant Price Taylor enters and offers a job to Cheyenne and Fuzzy. He shows the duo a paper called the *Vigilante* which boasts of attacks on his shipments, so they agree to help.

The next day Fuzzy is attacked as he drives a Taylor supply wagon. His partner runs the men off, but another group attacks. Cheyenne trails and catches one of the men, Abby's dad Frank Jackson, after he has given the goods to Bert and Elly.

Jackson is jailed and put in the same cell as the other outlaws. Taylor arrives to commend Cheyenne for catching the men he claims to boss. Cheyenne rides out to question Abby but is turned away after a rider informs her that Cheyenne caused her dad to be jailed.

The sheriff won't allow Abby or Cheyenne to see Jackson, claiming a court order is needed. Cheyenne and Fuzzy go to get one but hear gunshots and return to the jail. They find Jackson dead, the other jailed men gone, and the sheriff claiming to have shot Jackson as he tried to escape. The trio chases the three escapees but turn back when the barely-wounded sheriff claims to be hurt more seriously.

That night Cheyenne and Fuzzy go to Jackson. Their findings and Cheyenne's examination of the body earlier convince them that the sheriff has lied about the shooting.

Unable to get answers from townsfolk, Cheyenne dons a mask and takes goods to Bert and Elly. He learns that the sheriff and Taylor are in cahoots to maintain Taylor's monopoly and that Jackson helped to form the

Fuzzy St. John is reluctantly restrained by partner Lash LaRue as crooked sheriff Lee Morgan observes in *The Fighting Vigilantes.*

A disgusted Fuzzy St. John ignores the laughs of Jennifer Holt and Lash LaRue in a scene from *The Fighting Vigilantes.*

Fuzzy St. John is the target of the laughs of Lash LaRue and Jennifer Holt at the conclusion of *The Fighting Vigilantes.*

vigilantes to help the settlers.

Cheyenne shows Abby his marshal's badge and asks her help in bringing the guilty parties to justice.

After telling Taylor that Abby is behind the paper called the *Vigilante* and that she would be printing a copy that night, Cheyenne is not surprised when the sheriff arrives to take the printing press. Cheyenne informs him that he has bought it, so the sheriff leaves. Check and Shanks return to forcibly take the printing press but are turned back. Check escapes, but Shanks admits that the sheriff and Taylor are partners.

Cheyenne and Fuzzy arrive for a showdown at sunup and manage to beat back the challenge of Taylor's gang with blazing six guns and the help of Abby and the townsfolk. Now alone, the outlaw boss falls easy prey to Cheyenne, who uses his bullwhip to end Taylor's monopoly plans and threat to Abby and the Fighting Vigilantes.

* * *

Cheyenne Takes Over

58 Mins .... Oct. 25, 1947

Lash LaRue .... Cheyenne Davis
Fuzzy St. John .... Fuzzy Q. Jones
Nancy Gates .... Faye Wilkins
George Chesebro .... Wayne Dawson
Lee Morgan .... Delhaven
John Merton .... Bart McCord
Steve Clark .... Sheriff
Bob Woodward .... Jim Anderson
Marshall Reed .... Lawyer
Budd Buster .... Lem Boswick
Carl Matthews .... Messenger
Dee Cooper .... Player

Brad Slaven .... Bailey

Director .... Ray Taylor
Asst. Director .... Ira Webb
Producer .... Jerry Thomas
Screeplay .... Arthur E. Orloff

Cheyenne Davis and Fuzzy Q. Jones arrive at the ranch of Fuzzy's long-time friend Steve Lobos where his partner Cheyenne has been ordered to take a well-deserved rest. When they arrive, they are rebuffed by foreman Bart McCord who levels a rifle at them after telling them that Lobos is dead. Cheyenne whips the rifle from his hand and bests him in a fight.

The vacationing lawmen go to the Rock Creek Saloon for information on Fuzzy's friend and learn from the sheriff that the very profitable El Lobos Ranch is now run by Chicagoan Wayne Dawson to whom it was willed.

They return to the ranch to solve the mystery and are hired by Dawson as ranch hands.

Later that evening they go back to the saloon and question owner Faye Wilkins about the ranch because she became somewhat upset during their first visit when they mentioned the ranch by name. They learn that six months earlier Dawson entered her saloon with a lawyer whom he argued with and eventually killed. He threatened to kill Faye if she told of the after-hours killing of the man he claimed was a crook trying to take over his ranch.

Cheyenne and Fuzzy break into the ranch to look for the will. After leaving, they intercept a letter intended for Dawson and assure the messenger they will deliver it. The letter reveals that Dawson's brother Matt, whom he has not seen since youth, has died leaving him sole heir to the ranch.

In an effort to prove that Dawson is an impostor, Cheyenne identifies himself as a marshal to postmaster Jim Anderson and persuades him to deliver a substitute letter to Dawson. The letter informs Dawson that his brother will soon arrive.

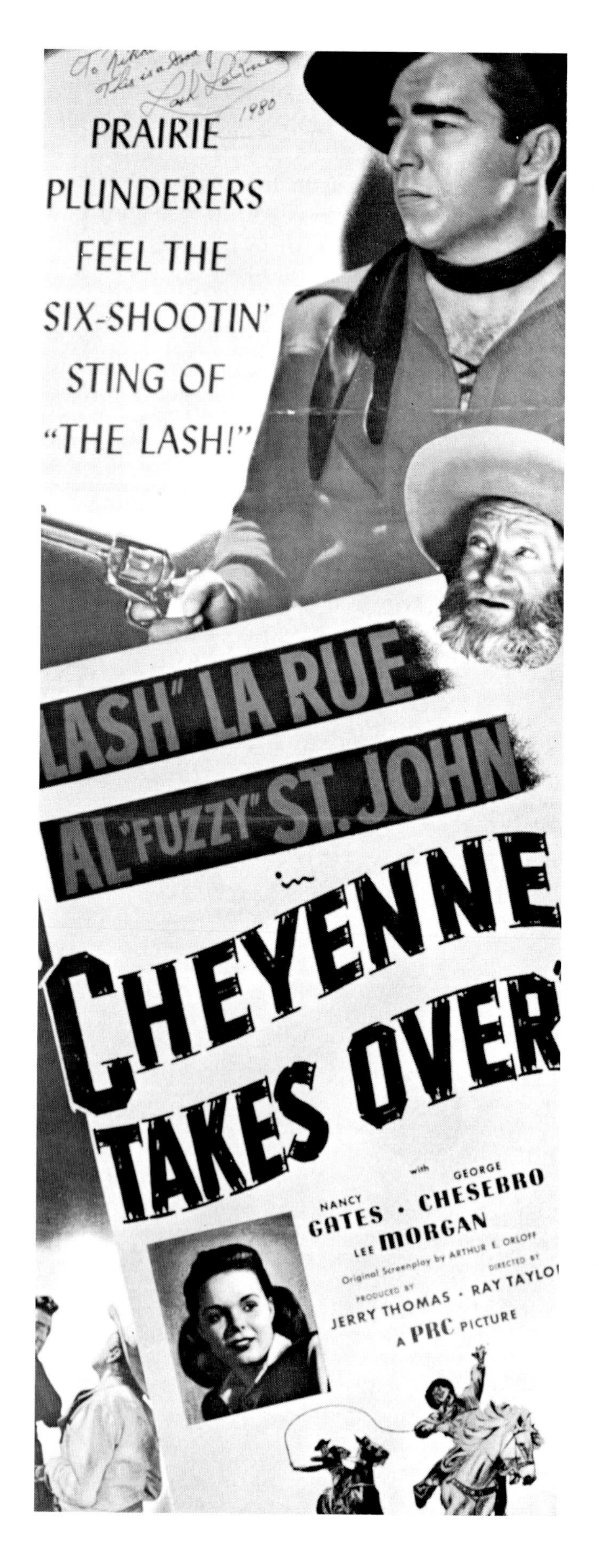

Lash and Fuzzy plan strategy in their attempt to thwart the outlaws. The scene is from *Cheyenne Takes Over.*

Faye assists Cheyenne by having a friend, Delhaven, masquerade as Matt using a special belt Cheyenne has had made by harness maker Lem Boswick.

Dawson and McCord wait to ambush Delhaven on the trail but flee when Cheyenne and Fuzzy approach. They give him the special belt and tell him what to do at the ranch.

When Delhaven meets Dawson, he asks about the matching belt he is supposed to have. Dawson claims it is being enlarged and goes to Lem's shop to have one made but is told it can't be made.

Cheyenne follows Dawson hoping he will dig up the body of the man he killed, the real Wayne Dawson, to get the fictitious belt. McCord intercepts Dawson after relieving Fuzzy of the real letter addressed to him. They search Delhaven's bags and learn he is an impostor and that Cheyenne is a marshal. McCord has Faye kidnapped.

Cheyenne trails Dawson, but McCord and his men are waiting nearby and a violent exchange of gunfire takes place. Fuzzy arrives with the sheriff, and Faye is rescued.

Cheyenne fights with the man masquerading as Dawson, in reality a crooked attorney. His foe escapes but is whipped from his horse and bested in the ensuing fight, thus ending Cheyenne's vacation.

* * *

Stage to Mesa City

55 Mins .... Nov. 1, 1947

Lash LaRue .... Cheyenne Davis
Fuzzy St. John .... Fuzzy Q. Jones
Jennifer Holt .... Margie Watson
Geroge Chesebro .... Padgett
Brad Slavin .... Bob Watson
Marshall Reed .... Allen Baxter
Terry Frost. .... Ed Williams
Carl Matthews .... Player
Bob Woodward .... Pete
Steve Clark .... John Watson
Frank Ellis .... Stocker
Lee Morgan .... Sheriff

Director .... Ray Taylor
Asst. Director .... Ira Webb
Producer .... Jerry Thomas
Screenplay .... Joseph F. Poland

Mesa City Stage Company owner John Watson, in financial trouble due to attacks on his line, learns (along with his lawyer Allen Baxter) that the postal inspector will arrive shortly to grant the mail contract.

Baxter, secretly behind the problems, orders henchmen Stocker to dry gulch Watson's daughter and son, Margie and Bob, who are on their way with money for the troubled line.

Cheyenne Davis and Fuzzy Q. Jones are enroute to Mesa City to investigate Watson's trouble when they see him shot by gunmen. Before dying, Watson asks the lawmen to ride out and meet Margie and Bob.

Margie and Bob are being shot at by bandits when Cheyenne and Fuzzy arrive

Lash rides into trouble on Black Diamond in this scene from *Stage to Mesa City.*

and trade gunfire with the evil doers and run them off. After identifying himself, Cheyenne tells Margie and Bob of their father's demise.

In Mesa City, Cheyenne is introduced as the Watson's business associate, so he can investigate without his marshal's identity being revealed. Baxter suggests that the line fold because of the attacks, but Cheyenne says no.

At the saloon, Bob recognizes bar patron Ed Williams as one of those in the attack. He is about to be shot when Cheyenne whips the gun from Williams' hand and bests him in a brawl.

Baxter tells Bob that an attack might be avoided if the stage takes off a day early. Cheyenne learns that Bob has taken Baxter's advice and follows. He finds the stage under siege and runs the attackers off. He escorts a wounded Bob back to town.

When Cheyenne learns from Fuzzy of Williams' visit to the sheriff, the lawmen follow him. He and his men meet Baxter and reveal to him that Cheyenne is a marshal. After being discovered, Cheyenne and his partner flee but are chased.

Cheyenne chases Baxter on horseback and then on foot. Baxter, preparing to confess after being captured, is shot by an unseen killer.

Town postmaster Padgett gives Margie a letter saying the postal inspector is on his way. She rides to meet his stage but instead meets trouble. Cheyenne rescues her but a shot from an unknown source rings out. The gunman escapes but loses a heel from his shoe.

Cheyenne questions wheelchair-con-

A dying Steve Clark asks Lash LaRue and Fuzzy St. John to not allow his son and daughter to be harmed in *Stage to Mesa City.*

Lash LaRue swaps lead with outlaws in *Stage to Mesa City.*

"STAGE
TO MESA
CITY"
"LASH" LA RUE • AL "FUZZY" ST. JOHN

"STAGE
TO MESA
CITY"
"LASH" LA RUE • AL "FUZZY" ST. JOHN

fined Padgett and discovers that the missing heel belongs to him. Padgett manages to flee from his office and ride away, but Cheyenne is close behind. Padgett is knocked from his horse after a long chase but is far from finished as he and Cheyenne become embroiled in a fistfight. Cheyenne wins the rough fight and escorts the outlaw boss to jail, his attempt to tie up the mail contract having failed.

Margie and Bob's Mesa City Stage Company receives the mail contract and Cheyenne departs leaving Fuzzy behind to run for sheriff.

* * *

Dead Man's Gold
60 Mins.....Sept. 10, 1948

Lash LaRue .... Lash LaRue
Fuzzy St. John .... Fuzzy Q. Jones
Peggy Stewart. .... June Thornton
Terry Frost. .... Joe Quirt
John Cason .... Matt Conway
Pierce Lyden .... Sliver
Lane Bradford .... Mayo Evans
Steve Keyes .... Morgan
Marshall Reed .... Stage Passenger
Britt Wood .... Bartender
Cliff Taylor .... Oldtimer

Director .... Ray Taylor
Producer .... Ron Ormond
Asso. Prods ....Ira Webb/June Carr
Story. Ron Ormond/Ira Well

At the request of a friend, Lash LaRue and partner Fuzzy Q. Jones arrive in Gold Valley to help solve a problem he is experiencing. Upon entering the local watering hole, they encounter Matt Conway and his

Lash LaRue in a publicity still from *Dead Man's Gold.*

men, Sliver and Morgan, shooting up the saloon and harassing patrons. Lash confronts them and manages to get the rowdies to leave.

Lash and Fuzzy go to Mayor Evans' office to get directions to Jim Thornton's ranch. Evans tells them how to get there but expresses surprise because he claims Thornton is a good friend who has never told him of any problems he is having.

On the road to Thornton's, Conway and his men jump Lash, who manages to hold his own until Morgan pulls a gun on him. Fuzzy shoots Morgan, enabling Lash to continue his fight with Conway. After besting his foe, Lash orders him away.

At the Thornton ranch that night Lash learns from June Thornton that her uncle has been missing for four days and that an important letter due from the Sacramento assayer's office has yet to arrive. Lash goes through some of Thornton's papers for clues and finds a gold nugget leading him to suspect foul play.

The next morning Lash and Fuzzy see Conway and Sliver cover up the mine entrance on Thornton's land. Lash searches the mine after they leave and finds not only more gold nuggets but also a murdered Jim Thornton.

Due to an earlier altercation with foreman Joe Quirt, Lash comes up with a plan involving June because he believes Quirt is somehow involved.

June rides into town and asks the Mayor if her uncle has told him of his gold strike. Evans confides to her that he was aware of the strike but that he told Thornton that the gold was worthless. June then tells him that she has a letter to mail to the assayer's office and leaves. She is watched by Quirt as she departs.

Lash LaRue scuffles with John Cason as Pierce Lyden (left) and Terry Frost (right) watch in *Dead Man's Gold*.

"DEAD MAN'S GOLD"

WITH

PEGGY STEWART · JOHN CASON · TERRY FROST

AND

LANE BRADFORD · PIERCE LYDEN · MARSHALL REED · STEVE KEYES · BRITT WOOD · CLIFF TAYLOR · BOB WOODWARD

PRODUCED BY **RON ORMOND** DIRI

ASSOCIATE PRODUCERS

IRA WEBB AND **JUNE CARR**

A WESTERN ADVENTURE

RELEASED BY **SCREEN GUILD**

Fuzzy and Lash on location in *Dead Man's Gold.*

John Cason believes he has the drop on Lash, but reliable Fuzzzy is really the one with the advantage.

Conway and Sliver fail in their attempt to ambush June when Lash and Fuzzy run them off. Later, Quirt tries to shoot Lash and June as they talk at the ranch. He flees but is cornered and pounded by Lash after a swap of lead.

Conway and Sliver rob the stage of the letter June mailed to Sacramento, but Lash and Fuzzy trail the bandits to town. Conway gives the letter to his boss, Evans, who then decides that he no longer needs his henchmen. Evans guns down Sliver and is about to do the same to his main henchman, Conway, when Lash and Fuzzy arrive. Evans makes a break to get away but is brought down by Lash with his bullwhip. The adversaries exchange blows, but the outlaw boss is no match for his black-clad foe.

With Evans jailed and his task now complete, Lash moves on but has Fuzzy stay behind to help June.

* * *

Mark of the Lash
60 Mins..Oct. 15, 1948

Lash LaRue .... Lash LaRue
Fuzzy St. John .... Fuzzy Q. Jones
Suzi Crandall .... Mary Phillips
Marshall Reed .... Lance Taggart
John Cason .... Colt Jackson
Tom London .... Lem Kimberly
Jimmie Martin .... Danny Phillips
Steve Dunhill .... Jeff
Lee Roberts .... Ace Talbert
Cliff Taylor .... Spade
Britt Woods .... Bartender
Jack Hendricks .... Player
Harry Cody .... Sheriff

Director .... Ray Taylor
Producer .... Ron Ormond
Assoc. Producers .... Ira Webb/June Carr
Story .... Ron Ormond/Ira Webb

Plagued by trouble, the citizens of Red

Rock anxiously await the new marshal sent for by Lem Kimberly. Discussing the recent hanging of an innocent citizen and the deaths of previous lawmen in Red Rock, townsfolk are rightfully pessimistic.

U.S. Marshal Lash LaRue is on his way to Red Rock when Colt Jackson, Ace Talbert, and Jeff, henchmen of Lance Taggart, gun down a man they believe to be the incoming marshal. The three outlaws ride off hell-bent-for-leather when they observe the presence of a man in black. The man in black checks the body of the dead man and finds papers showing him to be a territorial land agent on the way to see Danny Phillips to prove his water rights to property known as Stone Canyon Springs.

Danny and his sister Mary arrive in town to see Taggart who disputes his claim to Stone Canyon Springs, but Danny gets into an argument with Colt. Lash arrives just in time to whip the gun from Colt's hand. The

Lash LaRue and Jimmie Martin are ready for action, but a wounded Tom London sits back in *Mark of the Lash.*

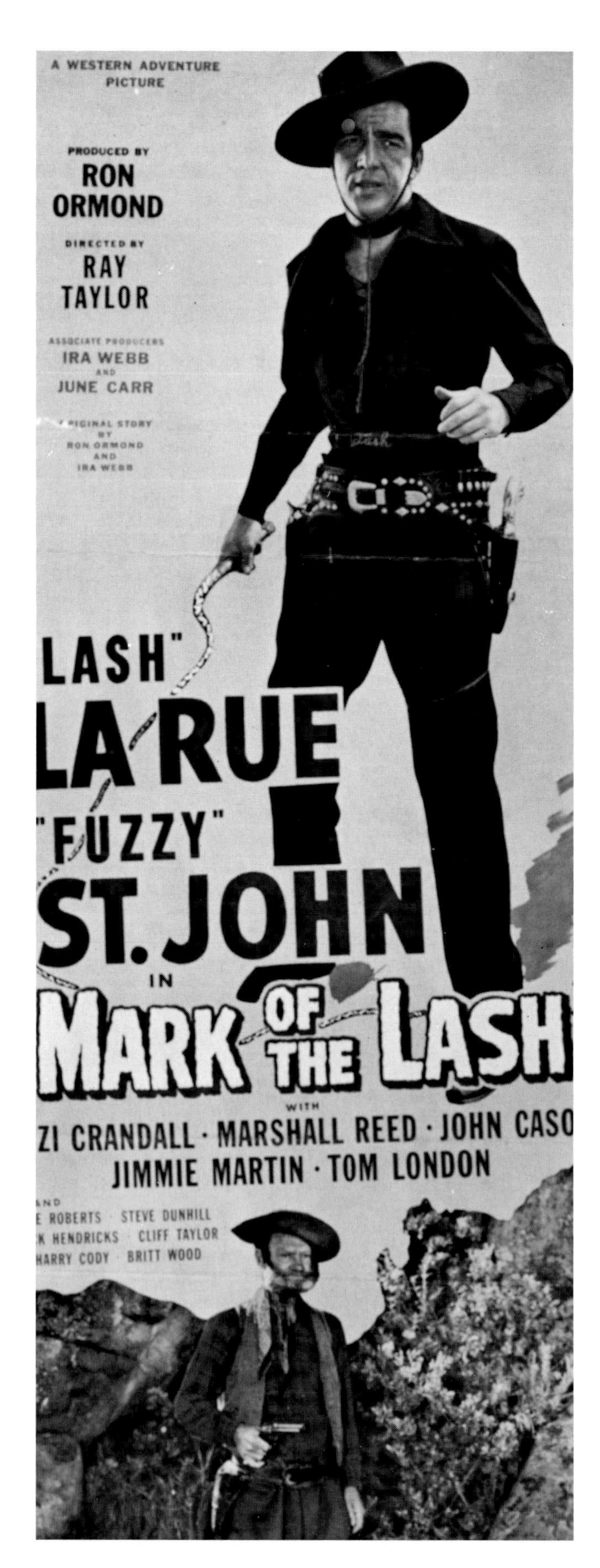

Marshall Reed takes a hard right from Lash LaRue in this scene taken from *Mark of the Lash.*

lawman then engages his adversary in a saloon-wrecking brawl. Papers belonging to the land agent fall to the floor during the fight and are picked up by saloon owner Taggart. After the fight, Taggart offers aid to Lash, presuming him to be the man his henchmen were sent out to kill. Lash goes along with the ruse.

Outside, Mary thanks Lash and offers room and board for him and his partner Fuzzy Q. Jones. She informs them that Taggart has fenced in the springs and now charges high rates for ranchers to water their cattle.

Taggart arrives at the Phillips ranch and informs Danny that 300 of his cattle have come onto his land and that he is there to collect for it. Ace and Danny trade punches, but Lash guns the henchman down when he is about to shoot his unarmed foe. Taggart claims to be acting sheriff and tells Lash that he must be put in jail by midnight for the killing.

Later, Kimberly arrives to inform Lash that Taggart and his men are holding a kangaroo court to try him and Danny. Fuzzy and Danny go with Kimberly while Lash heads for town. At the saloon, Lash reveals who he really is but is threatened by Colt and given until midnight to leave.

Lash and Fuzzy arrive later that night for a showdown. They are glad Danny and Kimberly have joined them when they find Taggart's men ready for action. Gunfire erupts from all directions. Danny and Kimberly are wounded, but Lash and Fuzzy are able to hold their own. Lash then meets Colt one-on-one and guns down his rugged foe.

The next morning Lash arrives to apprehend Taggart, but the debonair outlaw boss mounts his horse and tries to get away.

Lash whips him from his steed and pounds him into submission, completing his task.

With the question of the Phillips water rights answered, Lash and his bewhiskered sidekick prepare to depart Red Rock for adventures elsewhere.

* * *

Frontier Revenge

57 Mins.....Dec. 17, 1948

Lash LaRue	Lash LaRue
Fuzzy St. John	Fuzzy Q. Jones
Peggy Stewart	Joan DeLysa
Jim Bannon	Brant
Ray Bennett	Deuce Rago
Sarah Padden	Mrs. Owens
Jimmie Martin	Pete
George Chesebro	Col. Winston
Lee Morgan	Jake
Cliff Taylor	Bartender
Jack Hendricks	Red
Bud Osborne	Dawson
Forrest Mathews	Guard
Sandy Sanders	Bart

Director	Ray Taylor
Producer	Ron Ormond
Assoc. Producers	Ira Webb/June Carr
Screenplay	Ray Taylor

Lash LaRue and Fuzzy Q. Jones are dispatched to Raolite to combat the banditry in the area. They decide to masquerade as the notorious outlaws known as the Dawsons, whom Fuzzy has just apprehended.

Jake, Bart and Pete, henchmen of saloon owner Deuce Rago, are sent to waylay an incoming stage bearing the Silver Queen Mine payroll. Lash and Fuzzy are aware of

Jim Bannon's advances are not appreciated by Lash LaRue or Peggy Stewart in *Frontier Revenge.*

the payroll and decide to watch the stage. The outlaws attack, but the lawmen don masks and take the payroll, pretending to be outlaws themselves.

Rago and his right hand man Brant are upset at the failed holdup. Lash and Fuzzy arrive at Rago's saloon and are recognized as the men who waylaid the outlaws. Brant has Jake and Bart follow them when they make their exit. The elusive lawmen give them the slip with Lash whipping Bart from his horse and besting him in a fight while Fuzzy disarms Jake. The ruffians are tied to a tree and left.

Lash returns to the saloon and accuses Brant of having him tailed. After an exchange of punches, Brant leaves and Lash is summoned by Rago for a talk. Lash tells him that the Silver Queen is about to make a big shipment and that he will cut him in if he will personally assist in the hijack. Rago agrees.

The next morning Lash and Fuzzy run out on Rago's men when told by them that the boss would not be a party to the heist. Rago's men are unable to rob the wagon because Lash told the mine owner's to melt the silver into 250-pound units.

That evening singer Joan Delysa leaves the saloon for a breath of air. She is accosted by Brant, but Lash stops his unwelcome advances by besting him in a tough fight.

Rago calls Lash to his office to discuss the bungled hijacking and to talk him into a cut of the take that he and Fuzzy took from his men in the stage holdup. Lash offers to cut him in on the mine's big payroll haul if he will help this time. Rago agrees and Lash slips a note to Joan to warn the mine owner.

Rago goes along this time but has Brant take Lash off to force him to tell where the stage holdup money is hidden. Lash is tied to a tree and beaten by Brant who decides to shoot him after failing to get the information. Joan arrives to gun Brant down and then joins Lash in a search for his partner. Lash disarms Fuzzy's captor with his whip and then takes off for the mine.

Rago and his men succeed in taking the payroll and riding off, but Lash is in hot pursuit. Lash whips Rago's accomplice from his horse and then corners the outlaw boss. After a taste of the whip, Rago is ready to go to jail.

Joan, now revealed to be a lady agent, joins Lash and Fuzzy as they prepare to leave. On the way they discover Jake and Bart still tied to a tree. Realizing they can't read, Fuzzy frees them and gives them a note to give the sheriff, one which suggests they be hung on sight.

* * *

Outlaw Country

76 Mins..........................Jan. 16, 1949

Lash LaRue .... Lash LaRue
Lash LaRue .... The Frontier Phantom
Fuzzy St. John .... Fuzzy Q. Jones
Dan White .... Jim McCord
John Merton .... Marshal Clark
Nancy Saunders....................... Jane Evans
Lee Roberts .... Buck
Bob Duncan .... Deputy
Sandy Sanders .... Deputy
Max Terhune, Jr ....Player
Steve Dunhill .... Turk
Ted Adams .... Frank Evans
Dee Cooper ....Jeff Thomas
House Peters, Jr ....Cal Sanders
Steve Keyes ....Player

Nancy Saunders and Ted Adams listen intently as Lash LaRue formulates a plan in *Outlaw Country.*

Lash LaRue has a confrontation with Dan White (center) while masquerading as The Frontier Phantom. Lee Roberts (right) and Steve Dunhill look on in *Outlaw Country.*

The bullwhip was his trademark, and he could use it well.

Cast, crew, and an assortment of others on the set of *Outlaw Country.* Man seated in front of Fuzzy St. John must be his double.

Jack O'Shea .... Senor Cordova

Director .... Ray Taylor
Producer .... Ron Ormond
Assoc. Prods .... Ira Webb/June Carr
Screenplay............. Ron Ormond/Ira Webb

Lash LaRue and Fuzzy Q. Jones arrive in the ghost town of Fork River to receive their next job orders from Marshall Clark. After besting Cal Saunders and two other deputies unknowingly pitted against him to prove his toughness, Lash and Fuzzy are ordered across the border to rescue kidnapped U.S. engraver Frank Evans from a gang of counterfeiters that includes Lash's twin brother, The Frontier Phantom.

Enroute to Robbers Roost, Lash and Fuzzy see outlaws chasing Evans and his daughter Jane. The Phantom escapes, but his partners, Buck and Turk, are waylaid by Lash and Fuzzy. Fuzzy is left to watch the fallen outlaws while Lash leads Evans and Jane to safety.

Lash returns to get Fuzzy but finds a note from the Phantom indicating that Fuzzy has been taken to Robbers Roost and ordering him to depart.

Lash goes to the deserted shack to tell Evans what has happened but instead comes face to face with the Phantom. Lash is glad to hear that his brother would quit the gang if he were not in so deep, but their talk leads to a fight which Lash is able to win. Lash dons his brother's clothes and leaves him with Evans and Jane before going to get Fuzzy.

Disguised as the Phantom, Lash arrives in time to rescue Fuzzy, who is about to be shot by Turk after losing much money to him in a card game. Buck and Turk are suspicious of this action and go tell McCord.

McCord meets with Lash and tells him to bring in Evans and Jane. The outlaw boss is also suspicious because he is unable to get a cigar from the usually cigar-laden Phantom.

Still disguised as the Phantom, Lash leaves Robbers Roost only to be trailed by

Buck and Turk. Lash tricks them and then knocks Turk from his horse with a well-timed right before whipping Buck from his steed and beating him to the draw. Turk comes to and overhears Lash talking to Fuzzy who has arrived on the scene. He then rides back to tell McCord.

Fuzzy later meets the Phantom dressed as Lash. He apprises the Phantom of the situation and rides on while the Phantom heads to help out Lash.

Lash arrives at Robbers Roost and is accused by McCord of being an impostor and a lawman. He is then surrounded by armed men but help in the form of the Phantom arrives and the brothers battle McCord's men in a furious gun battle.

Fuzzy arrives just in time with a posse

as the Phantom is wounded and the outlaws are about to close in on Lash. McCord manages to flee but is brought down by the bullwhip and is pummeled into submission by Lash.

Marshal Clark prepares to take the wounded Phantom off to jail but assures all that since he helped mark the counterfeit bills and helped to fight the gang that only a light sentence is in order.

* * *

Son of Billy the Kid

65 Mins..March 6, 1949

Lash LaRue .... Jack Garrett
Fuzzy St. John .... Fuzzy Q. Jones
June Carr .... Betty Raines
Johnny James .... Colt
Marion Colby .... Norma Barry
Terry Frost .... Cy Shaeffer
George Baxter .... Jim Thorn
House Peters, Jr .... Outlaw
Clark Stevens ....Outlaw
Stan Jolley .... Matt Fergus
Eileen Dixon .... Dance Hall Girl
Bob Duncan .... Clem Yantis
Cliff Taylor .... Jake
William Perrott........................ Billy the Kid
Rosa Turich .... Rosa
Jerry Riggio ....Sanchos
Felipe Turich .... Jose
and Bud Osborne, Felice Richmond

Director .... Ray Taylor
Producer .... Ron Ormond
Assoc. Prods .... Ira Webb/Jane Carr
Screenplay............. Ron Ormond/Ira Webb

U.S. Marshal Jack Garrett prevents the holdup of the Baldwin City Stage while enroute to see town banker Jim Thorn. It so happens that Thorn is a passenger on the stage which is escorted safely to town after Garrett drops a couple of the masked men.

Outlaws House Peters, Jr. (left) and Bud Osborne are not too pleased with whip-wielding Lash LaRue in this publicity shot from *Son of Billy the Kid.*

Outlaws Colt and Fergus inform Cy Shaeffer, their boss, of the black-clad stranger's intervention. They are told to eliminate him and that help is coming from Clem Yantis, who is enroute to help Shaeffer in his quest to buy all lands in the area.

Garrett informs Thorn that his bank has been selected to handle the cash funds of the incoming railroad and that further robbery attempts are to be expected.

Yantis arrives and is ordered by Shaeffer to rob Thorn's bank, since his men failed to heist the money he brought in to help the troubled landowners. The bank robbery fails when Yantis and his men find that someone dynamited and emptied the bank safe before their arrival. Shaeffer asks Yantis to lie low until he learns when the railroad money will come.

The next morning, after informing Thorn and his niece Norma Barry, who is also his secretary, that the railroad money is coming by prairie schooner, Garrett, accompanied by Baldwin City sheriff Fuzzy Q. Jones, goes to meet the shipment. He and Fuzzy spot a hard-riding man and trail him to a deserted shack. When he leaves the shack, Garrett goes to investigate. After knocking out the guard, he searches the shack and locates a note indicating that the outlaws know of the shipment too.

Garrett and Fuzzy warn the schooner driver to expect trouble. The outlaws prepare to strike but decide to wait until the money makes it to Thorn's bank.

Yantis visits Thorn and reveals to him that he knows him to be former outlaw Billy the Kid and that gang member Colt is his son. Thorn promises to deliver the money to Yantis when he threatens to harm Colt.

Thorn tells Garrett and Fuzzy to meet him later at Boulder Pass. As he puts the money back in the safe, Norma pulls a gun and reveals that she is Yantis' accomplice. Colt arrives and disarms her, so Thorn goes on to Boulder Pass.

Yantis and his men attack a wagon they believe is bringing the money but find it full of gunmen. Thorn and Colt arrive and help Garrett and Fuzzy battle the outlaws. Colt guns down Yantis, causing outlaw boss Cy Shaeffer to flee. Garrett chases him and brings him down with his bullwhip. A vicious fight takes place which Garrett wins when his opponent topples to his death from the cliff on which they were fighting.

Garrett reveals that he suspected Norma, since the note in the outlaw's shack was in shorthand. Thorn admits that he is Billy the Kid and that Colt joined the gang to protect him. It turns out that Colt dynamited the safe to prevent the holdup. Garrett assures Thorn that the government will probably go easy on him since he helped wipe out the outlaw gang.

* * *

Son of a Badman
64 Mins..April 2, 1949

Lash LaRue .... Lash LaRue
Fuzzy St. John .... Fuzzy Q Jones
Michael Whalen .... Harlow Jarvis
Noel Neill .... Vicky
Jack Ingram .... Rocky
Zon Murray .... Leo Horn
Francis McDonald .... Joe Christ
Don Harvey .... Sheriff Rago
Frank Lackteen .... Piute
Edna Holland .... Mrs. Burley
William Bailey .... Brad Burley
Doye O'Dell .... Tex James
Sandy Sanders .... layer
Steve Raines .... Larson
Chuck Cason .... Bart

Director .... Ray Taylor
Producer .... Ron Ormond

His mask meant REVENGE!
His knife meant DEATH!
Lash
LA RUE
Fuzzy
ST. JOHN
IN
SON of a BADMAN
WITH MICHAEL WHALEN
NOEL NEILL · ZON MURRAY
JACK INGRAM · STEVE RAINES
CHUCK CASON · DON HARVEY
Producer
RON ORMOND
Associate Producer
Ira Webb and June Carr
Director – RAY TAYLOR
Original screenplay by Ron Ormond and Ira Webb
A WESTERN ADVENTURE PRODUCTION
Released by SCREEN GUILD PRODUCTIONS

Fuzzy St. John's worrisome tooth leads him and partner Lash LaRue to a confrontation with the *Son of a Badman.*

Fuzzy St. John and Lash LaRue are surprised to find Frank Lackteen and Noel Neill at the Indian Stockade in *Son of a Badmen.*

Assoc. Prods .... Ira Webb/June Carr
Screenplay.............. Ron Ormond/Ira Webb

Lash LaRue and Fuzzy Q. Jones are enroute to Star City in answer to a letter from Brad Burley when they encounter a riderless horse. A few feet away they find the rider—Brad Burley—dead from a knife wound. The lawmen continue their journey only to be set upon by Rocky, Leo Horn, and Bart, henchmen of masked bandit El Sombre. After swapping lead and punches with their adversaries, they are able to get away.

In Star City a reluctant Fuzzy is escorted to town dentist Dr. Harlow Jarvis because of a worrisome toothache, while Lash visits the sheriff. Lash introduces himself as a lawman to Sheriff Rago and tells him of the trouble he experienced on the trail and the discovery of the body of Brad Burley. The sheriff agrees to check into the matter.

Lash and Fuzzy are about to leave for the Burley ranch when they see Horn and Rocky ride off. They decide to follow them, and while so doing, they spot El Sombre and the sheriff at different spots along the trail. When the lawmen split up, Fuzzy is captured by Rocky, but Lash gives Horn the slip. Lash is able to rescue his sidekick who then hauls Rocky off to jail.

At the Burley ranch, Lash learns from Mrs. Burley that her husband and Joe Christ, representative of a group buying up land in the area, recently argued over the valuable property at the Indian Stockade. Burley had agreed to sell the property to him but later willed it to his niece Vicki instead.

That night Lash and Fuzzy watch the jail, believing that Rocky will be let loose by the sheriff. Their hunch is right, so they trail Rocky and Horn as they head to the Indian Stockade. When the outlaws leave the

Lash LaRue and George J. Lewis square off as Fuzzy St. John keeps everything honest in *King of the Bullwhip.*

stockade, Lash and Fuzzy prepare to search for clues but are interrupted by Vicki and Piute, her Indian sidekick. As they talk, outlaw boss El Sombre rides up, fires at them and then rides off hastily.

After selling the stockade to Christ at Lash's suggestion, Vicki, Lash, and Fuzzy watch the stockade to see what happens. They notice that the new owner has erected a sign of exorbitant toll charges for road usage there.

Mrs. Burley informs Christ that her niece is a minor and that a new bill of sale must therefore be drawn up. As Christ is about to sign, his boss El Sombre arrives and knifes him because he believes he has been crossed. Lash and Fuzzy arrive, but the masked man escapes by using Vicki as a shield.

After learning from Mrs. Burley that Dr. Jarvis' father, outlaw Apache Jack, had been hanged years earlier by area vigilantes, Lash believes him to be El Sombre and pays him a visit. Lash complains of a toothache and pretends to be knocked out by strong medicine given him by Dr. Jarvis. The doctor dons his mask and costume and departs.

Lash chases his quarry and whips the surprised man from his steed. After he soundly thrashes the masked villain, Lash hauls him off to jail, putting an end of the treachery of the Son of a Badman.

* * *

King of the Bullwhip

59 Mins .... Feb 1, 1951

Lash LaRue .... Lash LaRue
Fuzzy St. John .... Fuzzy Q. Jones
Jack Holt .... James Kerrigan
Tom Neal .... Benson
Anne Gwynne .... Jane Kerrigan
George Lewis ....Rio

Michael Whalen .... Thurmond
Dennis Moore .... Joe Chester
Mary Lou Webb .... Mary Lou
Willis Houck .... Player
Cliff Taylor .... Mr. Palmer
Frank Jaquet .... Bartender
Tex Cooper .... Buffalo Bill
Hugh Hooker .... Player
Jimmie Martin .... Pizor
Roy Butler .... Tom Powers
Ray Hughes .... Player

Director .... Ron Ormond
Producer .... Ron Ormond
Assoc. Prod .... Ira Webb
Story .... Jack Lewis/Ira Webb

The Tioga Cattlemen's Association, under constant threat from a masked whip-wielding bandit called El Azote, learns from president James Kerrigan that the marshal's office has sent out its two top men, Lash LaRue and Fuzzy Q. Jones to fight the bandit.

Enroute to Tioga City, Lash and Fuzzy are set upon by bullet-tossing desperadoes but manage to elude them and arrive safely.

Fuzzy enters the saloon and gets into trouble right away with Rio and Thurmond, hirelings of saloon owner Benson. Lash rescues Fuzzy but precipitates a brawl with Rio. After he bests Rio, Lash gets an apology from Benson. Lash tells him that the outlaws attempted to jump him and Fuzzy, and that they found two dead lawmen and buried them.

Having planted the idea that the lawmen were killed, Lash and Fuzzy take their horses to the stable. Rio and his men arrive bent on revenge and decide to hang Lash and Fuzzy. Kerrigan and Joe Chester, his bank cashier, hear the commotion and go in to break it up. Lash tells them the story about the murdered lawmen too, as Benson arrives and runs his men off.

Benson, having noticed the bullwhip Lash carries, offers him a job masquerading

George J. Lewis temporarily has the upper hand on Lash LaRue in an action scene from *King of the Bullwhip.*

Here is a rare photo from *King of the Bullwhip.* Lash is wearing the costume of the (normally masked) whip-wielding bandit, El Azote. Lash explained that he played the villain in some scenes of the movie and that sometimes he was actually fighting against himself.

as El Azote to cut in on his robberies. Lash and Fuzzy go along with Benson and help on many holdups, figuring to regain all of the stolen monies later.

On a job Lash and Rio have a dispute when the outlaw is about to shoot an innocent man. Lash uses his whip to persuade Rio. Benson orders Lash to lie low for a while.

The real El Azote continues his attacks. Lash confronts Benson and accuses him of working for El Azote while Fuzzy holds Rio and Thurmond at bay. Benson is about to talk after being roughed up by Lash, but Rio arrives with guns drawn to stop him after overpowering Fuzzy. Lash and his partner are tied up.

Rio and his men decide to rob the bank before leaving town. After getting free, Lash prevents the holdup with gun and whip, but he and Jane, Kerrigan's daughter, are prevented from putting away the bank's money by El Azote who comes in, takes the money, and hurriedly rides away.

Lash takes off after the masked bandit. After a long chase, El Azote is trapped but now more dangerous as he pulls out his bullwhip and takes on his adversary in a tremendous battle. The bullwhip fight is a lengthy one with each man receiving several lashes. At one point El Azote loses his whip but has it returned to him so the combatants can continue. Lash emerges victorious in the bullwhip fight and the brief fisticuff battle which follows. The mask is torn from the face of El Azote to reveal none

J. FRANCIS WHITE and JOY HOUCK PRESENT
THE DALTONS' WOMEN
"I'VE GOT MY BRAND ON YOU"
WITH
TOM NEAL
PAMELA BLAKE
JACK HOLT
LASH LARUE · FUZZY ST. JOHN
AND
RAYMOND HATTON · LYLE TALBOT
JACQUELINE FONTAINE · JUNE BENBOW
ARCHIE TWITCHELL · DUKE JOHNSON
J. FARRELL MacDONALD
—2 Song Hits—
"THE RIGHT KIND OF LOVE"
(MUSIC & LYRICS BY PETE GATES)
"DO IT OVER AND OVER AGAIN"
(LYRICS BY RENE LaMARRE
MUSIC BY FRANK ANDERSON
AND RONALD BADGER)
—PLUS 7 OTHER MUSICAL HITS—
"FOR MY MAN... I'D KILL YOU!... OR HIM."
Produced by RON ORMOND
Directed by THOMAS CARR
Associate Producer: IRA WEBB
WRITTEN FOR THE SCREEN BY MAURICE TOMBRAGEL AND RON ORMOND
A WESTERN ADVENTURE PRODUCTION

other than bank cashier Joe Chester, a dangerous foe but no match for the King of the Bullwhip.

With law and order now restored to the people of Tioga City, Lash and Fuzzy prepare to depart.

* * *

The Daltons' Women

80 Mins .... Feb. 25, 1951

Lash LaRue .... Lash LaRue
Fuzzy St. John .... Fuzzy Q. Jones
Jack Holt .... Mike Leonard
Tom Neal .... Mayor
Pamela Blake .... Joan Talbot
Jacqueline Fontaine ....Jackie
Raymond Hatton .... Sheriff
Lyle Talbot ....Jim Thorn
Tom Tyler .... Emmett
J. Farrell MacDonald.......................... Alvin
Terry Frost .... Billy Saunders
Stanley Price .... Manson
and Bud Osborne, Cliff Taylor, Buff Brady, Clarke Stevens, Lee Bennett, Jimmie Martin, Archie Twitchell

Director .... Thomas Carr
Producer .... Ron Ormond
Assoc. Prod .... Ira Webb
Screenplay.......... Maurice Tombragel, Ron Ormond

Marshal Lash LaRue and his deputy Fuzzy Q. Jones arrive in Navajo to rid the town of its lawlessness. Lash is able to remain undercover because he is hired by sa-

On the set of *The Daltons' Women:* (left to right) Fuzzy St. John, Jay N. Houck, Jack Holt, J. Francis White, Pamela Black, Lash LaRue, and an unidentified dignitary.

Another "behind the scenes" photo from *The Daltons' Women:* (left to right) Jay N. Houck, Lash LaRue, J. Francis White, and Fuzzy St. John.

loon owner Mike Leonard (alias Clint Dalton) to replace the house dealer Lash has just caught cheating.

Singer Joan Talbot, secretly a Pinkerton Detective, tells Lash of a robbery that she has heard is about to take place. Sure enough, that evening the bank is robbed of $40,000.

Having seen Leonard and cohort Manson leave the bank, Lash puts on a mask and goes to banker Jim Thorn and tells him and the mayor that he believes Leonard to be the robber.

Thorn and the crooked sheriff go to search Leonard's safe but find it empty because Leonard has transferred the stolen money to a wall safe. Thorn leaves in disgust but is stopped by a bar patron who tells him that Lash was absent during the theft and that he is probably the guilty party. Lash is accused of being Jess Dalton and is about to be a jail guest, but Fuzzy helps him to get away.

Joan finds Lash and Fuzzy at a deserted cabin later and informs them that some of the Daltons are working on the Manson ranch. Billy Saunders alias Jess Dalton sees Joan at the cabin and trails her back to the saloon, where he warns Leonard about her activities.

Joan discovers the hidden wall safe and returns to tell Lash that the stolen money is probably hidden in it. Lash tells Joan to remain at the cabin while he heads for town. Saunders follows him; they trade gunfire, and Lash catches and bests him in a brutal fight.

Lash dons the mask again before returning to Thorn's. He turns a cache of loot over to Thorn that he took from outlaws in an earlier heist to hopefully convince him of his innocence. The mayor and Alvin are also present at this encounter but when Lash leaves, the mayor, a Leonard cronie, leaves and informs his boss of what has transpired.

Saunders escapes from the cabin where he was held and joins Leonard and other Dalton hirelings in a bank heist before leaving town. The safe is opened, but Fuzzy jumps out and tosses lead at the hoodlums. Thorn and Alvin enter from a back room and help round up the gang, but leader Leonard manages to escape.

Leonard flees to the stable where he attempts to mount his horse and leave town, but he forgets to count on opposition from a whip-wielding Lash, who whips a gun from Leonard's hand before besting him in a tough fight.

Thorn and Alvin thank Lash, Fuzzy, and Joan as they are about to leave, but a delay is in order—a kiss from Joan floors a surprised Fuzzy.

* * *

The Thundering Trail

55 Mins .... Aug. 1, 1951

Lash LaRue .... Lash LaRue
Fuzzy St. John .... Fuzzy Q. Jones
Sally Anglim .... Betty Jo
Archie Twitchell .... Tom Emory
Ray Bennett .... Ed West
Sue Hussey .... Sue
Mary Lou Webb .... Miss Smith
Clarke Stevens .... Clarke
John Cason .... Conway
Jimmie Martin .... Clinton
George Chesebro .... Charlie Jones
Ray Broome .... Bartender
Johnny Howard .... Player
Cliff Taylor .... Moore
Bud Osborne .... Joe
Doris Hart. .... Player
Ruby Couch .... Player

Director .... Ron Ormond
Producer .... Ron Ormond
Assoc. Prod .... Ira Webb
Screenplay .... Ira Webb/June Carr

A new wave of violence and the concern of law-abiding citizens have caused the President to appoint a territorial governor to take care of the problems in a swift manner.

Tom Emory has been selected as governor but must now be escorted to Capitol

City to take office. To see to it that he arrives safely, Marshal Lash LaRue is dispatched but runs into trouble right away. Conway, a henchman of businessman Ed West, spots a rider on the trail and takes after him with two other outlaws, assuming him to be the marshal coming to assist Emory. Lash rides after the lead-tossing riders and runs them off but not before they have killed their prey, an innocent cattle buyer.

Lash arrives in town and meets his assistant Fuzzy Q. Jones at the stage depot. Operator Charlie Jones informs Lash that Emory and his niece Betty Jo will be in danger if they leave their ranch.

Conway reports to West that the man who ran them off has just entered the stage depot by the back door. Aware now that the wrong man was killed, West sends Conway and his men to prevent Lash from reaching Emory.

Lash and Fuzzy split up in case of trouble. Conway and his cronies jump Lash and knock him from his horse. Lash bests the trio with his fists but is about to be shot when Fuzzy arrives to save him. Lash and Conway resume their fight, but the outlaw is beaten again and then ordered off by Lash.

At the Emory ranch Lash and Fuzzy devise a plan to get Emory safely to Capitol City. Clarke, the deaf and dumb servant of Emory, is not what he seems and rides to warn his boss of what he has overheard.

The next day Fuzzy starts to drive Emory and Betty Jo to Capitol City by stage. The trip is barely underway when masked men toss lead at the stage. Lash, who is not far behind, catches the stage and transfers to it. His gunfire sends the bandits packing, and the trip continues. More bandits strike. They, too, are run off, but Lash feels it is best to turn back.

Another plan is devised, but Lash changes it after allowing Clarke to hear it,

Lash rarely got to kiss the girl in the movies. However, here is an exception in this scene from *The Thundering Trail.*

since he believes that he revealed the earlier plan.

Later, masked riders attack a covered wagon driven by Lash and Fuzzy because it is thought to conceal Emory. But the wagon hides several men who engage the bandits in a lengthy exchange of gunfire. A more-than-ample dose of lead poisoning causes them to flee.

Emory makes it safely to Capitol City and is installed as governor. Now in a position to realize his dream of a good life for citizens in the area, Emory tries to coax Lash into staying. He succeeds but only because his pretty niece Betty Jo decides to reward the black-clad man with a well-timed kiss—much to the amazement of Fuzzy.

* * *

The Vanishing Outpost

56 Mins..Nov. 1, 1951

Lash LaRue .... Lash LaRue
Fuzzy St. John. .... Fuzzy Q. Jones
Archie Twitchell .... Matt
Sue Hussey ....Sue
Sharon Hall .... Nancy Walker
Clarke Stevens .... Denton
Riley Hill ....Walker
Cliff Taylor .... Bartender
Ted Adams .... Deputy
Ray Broome ....Player
Bud Osborne .... Rufe
Lee Morgan .... Lou
Ned Roberts ....Player
Ray Jones ....Player
Curtis Rutledge ....Player

Director .... Ron Ormond
Producer .... Ron Ormond
Assoc. Prod .... Ira Webb
Screenplay. Maurice Tombragel, June Carr

Lash LaRue and his partner Fuzzy Q. Jones are headed North to clean up a couple of lawless towns when they decide to stop for the evening.

After tussling with Matt, a drunken bar patron, they prepare to settle down as Walker knocks on the door of their hotel room. Being a Pinkerton man, Walker recognizes Lash from an earlier job on which they worked and asks his aid in capturing the Taggart/Jackson gang that killed his partner the day before.

Lash is sent by Walker to intercept an outlaw message. After trailing the message bearer to a deserted shack and allowing him to leave, Lash overpowers a guard and searches the shack. His search is halted when he is warned by Fuzzy of an approaching rider.

Moments after Lash leaves, the cabin is overrun with outlaws. Lou, the man in charge, orders his men to go find those responsible for knocking out the guard and searching the cabin.

Four of the gunmen catch up with Lash and Fuzzy and dispense a hail of bullets their

Guard Bud Osborne is pummelled by Lash LaRue after first getting a taste of his whip in *The Vanishing Outpost.*

Riley Hill (second right) and Steve Dunhill (next to Lash) enjoy the antics of Fuzzy St. John in *The Vanishing Outpost.*

way. The lawmen split up and each is chased by two outlaws. Lash wounds one of his adversaries and whips the other from his horse. After besting the outlaw in a tough fight, Lash seeks Fuzzy. He finds him safe but a little sore after being dragged by the horse of his pursuer.

Walker meets Lash and Fuzzy later to get the message Lash found at the shack. Walker then asks that they deliver the message to his boss in Star City.

Before entering the place he is to meet Walker's boss, Lash is confronted by two ruffians. After taking them in a fight, he enters the building and meets Denton, Walker's boss. Denton assigns two deputies to accompany Lash and Fuzzy to Fall River to locate the Taggart/Jackson gang. He promises to send more help.

One of the deputies turns out to be in league with the outlaws. He warns two of his cohorts of Denton's plan and sends one of them to warn Jackson and Taggart.

Lash and Fuzzy arrive in the town of Fall River along with the two men who accompany them. A host of gunmen toss lead their way, but the lawmen are able to meet the challenge. Lash guns down Jackson, who makes the mistake of trying to outdraw him.

With Taggart still on the loose, Lash sends him a message by Fuzzy, asking that he give himself up. The outlaw boss refuses to give up.

Lash arrives at Taggart's saloon the next morning for a showdown. He trades lead with Taggart and then mounts up and chases him. Taggart is whipped from his horse and bested in a vicious fight.

Lash and Fuzzy depart for points north and more excitement.

* * *

IT TAKES A CROOK TO CATCH A CROOK!

"Lash" plays both sides of the law to do it!

Lash LARUE Fuzzy ST. JOHN

in The BLACK LASH

with PEGGY STEWART BYRON KEITH KERMIT MAYNARD BUD OSBORNE

Produced and Directed by RON ORMOND

The Black Lash
55 Mins..Jan. 2, 1952

Lash LaRue .... Lash LaRue
Fuzzy St. John .... Fuzzy Q. Jones
Peggy Stewart .... Joan DeLysa
Ray Bennett........................... Deuce Rago
Kermit Maynard .... Lem Woodruff
Byron Keith .... Bill Leonard
John Cason .... Cord
Clarke Stevens .... Johnson
Roy Butler.......................... Mayor Redfield
Larry Barton..................................... Judge
Johnny Howard ....Player
Bud Osborne .... Telegraph Operator
Jimmie Martin .... Pete
Johnny Paul.......................................Player
Smiley Wilson ....Player

Director .... Ron Ormond
Producer .... Ron Ormond
Assoc. Prod .... Ira Webb
Screenplay..... Timothy Ormond, June Carr

Fuzzy Q. Jones is in Danville awaiting word from his partner Lash LaRue, whom he has not heard from in three months. As he and the telegraph operator talk, word

Kermit Maynard restrains Fuzzy St. John after the latter broke in on a secret meeting with Lash LaRue in *The Black Lash.*

Lash LaRue shows Clarke Stevens his marshal's badge so they can prevent a gold hijacking attempt in *The Black Lash.*

Lash LaRue is roughed up by badman John Cason in a scene from *The Black Lash.*

comes that Deuce Rago is shipping a big load of cattle out of Raolite. Thinking Lash might be in Raolite, Fuzzy departs.

Rago, owner of the Union Saloon, and his attorney Bill Leonard are concerned over recent failures due to their inept men. Leonard suggests that they bring in heavy artillery to combat the problem. When Rago learns from his friend John DeLysa that a whip-wielding, black-clad man wearing a belt buckle bearing a "D" robbed his men of money they had taken from the stage, he realizes it is Lash and takes Leonard's advice to get him to help in future deeds.

Meanwhile Fuzzy seeks Lash at a shack they have used in the past and breaks in on him and Lem Woodruff, a detective with the land and cattle association. After informing Fuzzy that he and Lem robbed Rago's men, Lash and his bewhiskered partner leave to take the money to a friend for safekeeping.

Two of Rago's men spot Lash and Fuzzy and trail them. After a fight with Lash and Fuzzy, the henchmen are tied to a tree and left.

Lash goes for a meeting with Rago and agrees to help his men hijack a silver shipment that night. However, Lash tells Rago that since the split must be 50-50, the risk should be also and that he has to come along on the job.

That night the heist is about to take place when Rago's men tell Lash that Rago won't be coming. As a result, Lash and Fuzzy run out on the job. When the outlaws attempt the heist, they learn that the silver is in 250-pound units rather than the usual 25, and they are unable to take it. This scheme was devised by Lash who advised Silver Queen Mine foreman Johnson to ship in larger units to halt the robbery.

Lash and Fuzzy return to the saloon and learn from an apologetic Rago that the mine has a large payroll on hand just ripe for the picking, and this time he will join in on the job.

Lash and Fuzzy join Rago and his men

THE SHADOW OF DOUBT...
TWIN BROTHER PHANTOM
OR MARSHAL OF
THE LASH
J. FRANCIS WHITE & JOY HOUCK
Present
LASH LA RUE
FUZZY ST. JOHN
IN
THE FRONTIER PHANTOM
with ARCHIE TWITCHELL · VIRGINIA HERRICK
BUD OSBORNE · CLIFF TAYLOR
Produced and Directed by RON ORMOND
Associate Producer IRA WEBB
A WESTERN ADVENTURE
PRODUCTION

Kenne Duncan holds Fuzzy St. John at bay while Sandy Sanders does likewise to Lash LaRue in *The Frontier Phantom.*

to rob the mine of its payroll, but Rago has some of his men take Lash and Fuzzy off in an effort to force them to tell the location of the money they took in the stage incident. Lash is beaten up by Cord, but his partner rescues him after giving his captor the slip.

Lash goes to the mine, but Rago has the payroll and rides off. Lash is close behind as Rago reaches his office. Joan draws a gun on Lash, but Fuzzy rescues him again and the lawless are jailed. Fuzzy is made sheriff and Lash remains to help out.

* * *

The Frontier Phantom

56 Mins..............................Feb. 1. 1952

Lash LaRue .... Lash LaRue
Fuzzy St. John .... Fuzzy Q. Jones
Archie Twitchell .... Sheriff
Virginia Herrick ....Susie
Kenne Duncan....................... Sam Mantell
Sandy Sanders .... Outlaw
Clarke Stevens .... Deputy
Cliff Taylor...Sparky
Bud Osborne .... Matt
Buck Garrett .... Outlaw
Jack O'Shea ....Player
George Chesebro.......................Bartender
Smiley Wilson ....Player
Curtis Rutledge ....Player

Producer/Director .... Ron Ormond
Assoc. Prod .... Ira Webb
Screenplay. Maurice Tombragel, June Carr

U.S. Marshal Lash LaRue and his deputy Fuzzy Q. Jones are set for a meeting at midnight with notorious outlaw Sam Mantell at the Bird Cage Saloon. The meeting has been set up so that Lash, who is impersonating his hospitalized brother, the now-reformed Frontier Phantom and one-time Mantell associate, can capture and jail the noted criminal.

Matt and another deputy arrive at the shack at which Lash is hiding and arrest him believing him to be the real Frontier Phantom. Although Lash and Fuzzy attempt to explain what is going on, the deputies haul them off to Sawyer's Creek to the sheriff's office.

Lash tells his story to the sheriff at Sawyer's Creek, but it falls on deaf ears as the lawman claims it is too far-fetched to be true. The sheriff, however, decides to wire Tularosa to see if the sheriff there actually has identification papers for Lash and if the real Frontier Phantom is in fact in the hospital.

Only an hour remains until the scheduled meeting, but Lash uses it to tell the interested gathering the story of the Frontier Phantom and how he was able to infiltrate the Jim McCord gang and break it up since he and the Phantom, one of McCord's henchmen at the time, are twin brothers.

While the story is in progress, Sparky arrives to tell the sheriff that word has come in that Mantell and two of his men are headed to town. Because the sheriff remains unconvinced by Lash, the story is continued.

A short while later, Susie, the town wait-

Lash and Fuzzy seem to be snickering at the outcome of *The Frontier Phantom.*

"Shucks, I ran out of outlaws!"

ress, arrives with food as the story is being told. She tells the gathering that a bar patron saw Mantell and his men just outside of town.

With time running out and Lash still unable to convince all that he is a lawman, he does, however, manage to get the sheriff to agree to his plan. The sheriff is to put his men around the saloon and let Lash meet Mantell, but his men are to shoot the first man to emerge after the confrontation. Lash and the sheriff go to the saloon and ask the patrons to leave. Although he still doubts the story, the sheriff wishes Lash good luck before he also leaves the saloon.

At midnight Mantell and his men arrive. Lash confesses to Mantell that he is a lawman there to see to it that his outlaw days are a thing of the past. A shootout takes place in the dimly-lit saloon, but Lash and Fuzzy win out over the outlaws.

The sheriff arrives to lock up Mantell. He also plans to lock up Lash since word exonerating him has not come. A telegram comes just in time and all have a good laugh.

* * *

Chapter 4
From the Pages of Lash's Scrapbook

Lash LaRue and Smiley Burnette entertain children at the Faith Home Orphanage in Danville, Virginia. *(photo credit: Buddy Bryant)*

Lash LaRue and friend Clyde Carroll in a 1960s Atlanta, Georgia, photograph.

When Lash talked, the fans listened at the 1st Annual Memphis Film Festival. Boyd Magers (left) and Warren Chaney (center). Little Alan Magers is peering at the camera lens.

Awards ceremony at the legendary Peabody Hotel. (1972 Memphis Film Festival) (L to R): Don "Red" Barry, Sunset Carson, Sunset's friend, Russell Hayden, Jim Shoenberger, Lash, Max Terhune with Elmer.

No doubt Russell Hayden and Lash are talking about days gone by.

Fans at the 1972 Memphis Film Festival could not get enough of Lash's movie stories.

Three pals of the trail: Eddie Dean, Monte Hale, and Lash LaRue. (1974 Memphis Film Festival)

1974 Memphis Film Festival: Mike Mendozas, John Hagner, Lash LaRue, and a very happy Eddie Dean.

". . . and then I looked at him like this."

Lash never seemed to tire when he was around his fans regardless of how many questions they asked.

The crowd always gathered when Lash demonstrated his abilities with the bullwhip. (1974 Memphis Film Festival)

Lash and friends answered questions from the overflowing crowd at the Panel of the Stars: Eddie Dean, Dorothy Fay Ritter, moderator Jim Shoenberger, Jim "Red Ryder" Bannon, Johnny Bond, and Lash. (1974 Memphis Film Festival)

Lash accepted a special award at the Saturday night banquet. (1974 Memphis Film Festival)

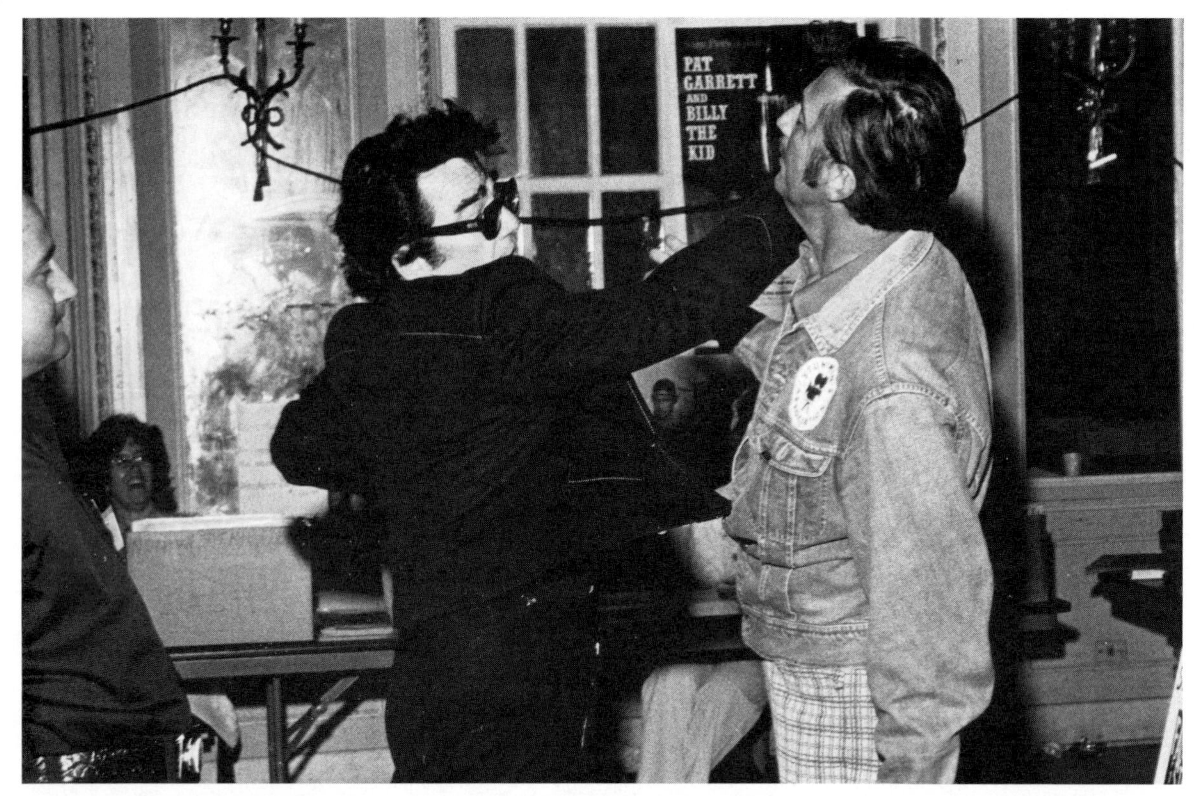

Lash demonstrated his stunt fighting ability to John Hagner, publisher of *Falling Stars,* for the fans' entertainment. (1974 Memphis Film Festival)

Lash entertained guests at the 1974 Memphis Film Festival awards banquet, along with show promoter Packy Smith and an unidentified fan.

King of the Bullwhip

An American Legend

Still Going Strong!

East Coast Office

H. D. MARTIN PRODUCTIONS

CHEROKEE FOOTHILLS SCENIC HIGHWAY NO. 11

GAFFNEY, SOUTH CAROLINA 29340

803-489-5201

The above newspaper advertisement appeared in the *Greensboro Daily News* in the early 1950s.

Reprinted from "People in the News," *Greensboro News & Record,* May 25, 1983.

Lash LaRue, who played the "Cheyenne Kid" several decades ago and used bullwhips that sometimes were 35 feet long, says he doesn't find security in his Social Security, and he's looking for work.

Nicknamed "King of the Bullwhip," La Rue was popular at the box office in the mid-1940s and early '50s.

Last week, he visited Conway, Arkansas, to negotiate with representatives of Castle Industries of Arkansas, Inc., a mobile home manufacturer, for public relations work.

"Being on Social Security is not so secure as people would think it would be, so I work, every once in a while, to supplement it," LaRue said.

Lash is back in the saddle again at Milo Holt's Old Time Western Film Club in Siler City, North Carolina.

" . . . and that's how I became a cowboy . . . ."

Lash with Pee Wee King (composer of "The Tennessee Waltz") at Charlotte's Western Film Fair.

"My eyes are not as good as they used to be, but here goes . . . ."

"Sure, I don't mind; one more photo can't hurt."

Lash gives the quiet sign to his granddaughter.

Many of Lash's friends, including Santa Claus, turned out to honor him at a special Christmas party in Spartanburg, South Carolina, on December 16, 1982.

Shawn Nix and Shon Greenlee posed with Lash at the Spartanburg, South Carolina, Christmas party. (December 16, 1982)

Even entertainer/author Jim Bob Tinsley was at the Christmas party.

"I'd like to thank all of you for honoring me tonight . . . ."

Reprinted from ***Greensboro News and Record*, November 21, 1984.**

Kernersville site of movie to star Lash LaRue

By SUSAN LADD
Staff Writer

KERNERSVILLE—

There was no mistaking Lash LaRue, famous for his starring roles in cowboy matinees of the '40s. Dressed in black with a silver horseshoe belt buckle, LaRue cut a dashing figure in the Kernersville courthouse.

LaRue, once known as the King of the Bullwhip, will return to films after a 30-year absence to star in "The Dark Power," the first feature of North Carolina filmmaker Phil Smoot.

LaRue will be the hero of the horror film. It's his first non-cowboy role.

LaRue's hair and beard are completely silver now, but the trim actor hasn't lost his touch. Even Major Roger Swisher jumped when LaRue, who is in his late 60s, cracked his whip.

At a press conference at the courthouse Tuesday, Smoot announced plans to shoot the suspense/thriller in Kernersville and Belews Creek. Filming begins Monday and continues through Dec. 22.

Smoot, an Asheboro native and graduate of the University of North Carolina at Chapel Hill, has worked for filmmakers Earl Owensby of Shelby and Bill Olsen of Hickory.

The $330,000 budget for "The Dark Power" is financed by Triad Motion Pictures Inc., a limited partnership of four investors: WTOB radio station manager David Plyler; Kernersville City Attorney John Wolfe; Kernersville accountant George Walker, and Smoot.

Smoot describes "The Dark Power" as a cross between "Halloween" and "My Favorite Year."

"It's a combination of the old and the new—we want to break a few rules," Smoot said. "Horror films of the past all took place in Europe. Ours is all-American, using American history. Usually everything happens in an old haunted house. Ours takes place in a new house where nobody's ever lived before. And instead of cringing in a corner, people are going to be fighting back."

The story is based on the legend of an Indian tribe whose members could bury themselves and come back alive, Smoot said. Makeup artist Tony Elwood displayed a number of grotesque masks to be used in the film.

Smoot said he met LaRue a year ago when the matinee star visited the set of a 3-D film Smoot was working on.

"We decided there were probably enough bad guys still around for him to make a come-back," Smoot said.

LaRue said he was looking forward to working in the Carolinas, where he has appeared at Western film conventions.

"It'll be the longest schedule I've ever worked on," LaRue said of the four-week shooting schedule. "In Hollywood, we did one a week. This is an epic for me."

Reprinted from *The Washington Times*, December 17, 1984

'The Dark Power'

Lash LaRue comes alive on the silver screen again

LaRue Stars Again

NAMES AND FACES

Al (Lash) LaRue, star of numerous 1940s cowboy movies, says he's excited about his first major role since the 1950s in a horror flick that will be filmed in Belews Creek and Kernersville, N.C. Shooting of "The Dark Power" is scheduled to begin Nov. 26 said producer and director Phil Smoot of Asheboro, N.C. who has worked in various capacities on 24 feature-length motion pictures. With the exception of a few minor walk-on parts, it will be LaRue's first movie role in more than 30 years, and his first in which he isn't playing a cowboy.

Lash is back

Lash LaRue, the whip-wielding star of Saturday matinee Westerns for an entire generation of movie-goers, isn't dead. And whoever said he was didn't talk to him first. Lash is back, and he's making a new movie—a monster film that features Lash in the biggest part in 30 years.

Lash LaRue Takes On The DARK POWER

by Frank Scott

KERNERSVILLE, N.C.—As the red Buick convertible moved slowly down the street, the tall, aging man in black waved to the crowd, acknowledging the cheers and occasionally responding to a comment from the throng.

It is an exceedingly rare event when anyone even remotely famous comes to this small town in North Carolina's Triad (Winston-Salem, Greensboro, High Point), but this time it was extra special. The man who had earned the place of honor in the Kernersville Christmas Parade—right behind mayor Roger Swisher—was not just anyone, he was a movie star. And not just any movie star, he was Lash LaRue—*Kernersville's* movie star.

Yes, Lash LaRue, hero of a hundred Saturday matinees. The not-quite-totally-good guy who used a bullwhip to bring the totally bad guys to justice. He didn't sing like Roy Rogers or Gene Autry; he just kissed the girl (lightly, in a polite sort of way), then rode off into the sunset.

But, the thought immediately comes to mind, that was 30 years ago. What is Lash LaRue doing in a small southern town's 1984 Christmas parade?

Well, 30 years after Lash LaRue last rode into the sunset, he has ridden back into the limelight. After all, "The Dark Power" has invaded Kernersville, and a hero is needed to save the town.

Reprinted from *The Blue Ridge Sun*, July 24, 1985.

Alleghany Is Tinsel Town - For Now!

Hollywood watch out, Alleghany is moving in! Yes, Alleghany has snatched a morsel of tinsel town fame! It is the location for filming "Alien Outlaw", a sci-fi old-west adventure film. The movie stars three old-west heroes from the days of Red Rider, with Alleghany as the back drop. The bad guys don't wear black hats, they fly a UFO.

Alleghany is well on the way to silver screen fame, with filming of the movie in progress. Shooting will continue through August 17th, according to Triad Motion Pictures, Inc, and Alpine Productions, Ltd., the two companies producing the film. Most of the footage will be shot in Alleghany, some in Grayson and some in Winston-Salem.

Phil Smoot, writer and director of the film, stated last week, that Alleghany was chosen for several reasons. "We needed mountains, horses, a place to get away from traffic noises, woods, streams and a cooperative community," stated Mr. Smoot in a press conference the likes of which Sparta hasn't seen!"

The film will feature, along with Alleghany scenery, three western stars of days gone by and a budding heroine from Winston-Salem. Lash LaRue will co-star with Kari Anderson as the main character, er-good guys. There will also be appearances from Sunset Carson and Wild Bill Cody. Rounding out the cast of leading characters is Virginia Van Hampton's sleek black mare - the leading lady's mount, and 24 other minor characters.

Tom Burgiss, decked out in cowboy attire for the event, welcomed the film company and stars, on behalf of the Chamber of Commerce. "The Chamber was happy to show Mr. Smoot, in preliminary meetings, the scenery and facilities for his movie," stated Burgiss at the Press Conference. "The Chamber was concerned at first about the type of movie...X...R or what. But Mr. Smoot assured us that it would not be a sex movie because Lash LaRue was the main star!"

Mr. Smoot noted that some local people were being used, and one part was still to be cast for the movie. "We're using a local customer and others," stated Smoot. "And of course, you'll see us at the local restaurants and so forth." Mr. Smoot called the film a low budget one, which will cost between $600,000 and $1 million to produce.

The timetable for "Alien Outlaw" will be shooting through mid-August, post production work completed by November and release in March of 1986. Triad Motion Pictures, Inc., was chartered in 1983 and has one movie to their credit. The first movie, also starring Lash LaRue, was made in conjunction with New Vision Productions, Ltd. The film, called, "The Dark Power" should be completed this month.

"Alien Outlaw" is a rather unique movie with a rather unique plot. The heroine, Jesse Jamison, i.e., Kari Anderson on Virginia Van's horse, has an old-west gun show. The show isn't doing so hot and then the bad guys, the aliens appear on the scene. It seems they have crashed in the mountains and due to a lack of lasers or something they steal all of Jesse's guns. Well this will never do, because the aliens proceed to go people hunting. Since the local citizenry does not believe Jesse's story, she turns to old-time friend - Alex i.e., Lash LaRue. The two set out to rid the planet of the evil aliens and make the world once again safe for Democracy and two-bit old west shows. It's apparently a clever mixture of sci-fi suspense and old-west good guys against evil, set in the beautiful mountains of Alleghany!

Lash LaRue, Sunset Carson and Kari Anderson were all in Sparta last week for the big Press Conference. Lash stated he was looking forward to doing some real acting without his famous whip, which will be absent from the script. Sunset Carson said he was looking forward to working with Lash because they had never shot a film together. Kari Anderson, who was cast from a group of 250 aspiring starlettes for the part, was beside herself with excitement. "Oh the whole thing is amazing," stated Ms. Anderson last week. "I was so pleased even to be considered and when they called me back I was delighted," stated Anderson. "It's a great opportunity to work with such great people."

Anderson, who lives in Winston-Salem is billed by Triad as "a very versatile performer' who has "choreographed over 100 stage show." She has worked with Greg Thompson's Follies, appearing in Atlantic City, and with Shea's Theatre in Buffalo, New York. Kari currently hosts the "Racing With Roy Hill" program on WLXI-TV 61 in Greensboro.

Lash LaRue is famous for his black outfit and whip. His most popular westerns came out in the forties and fifties. Sunset Carson went from rodeo cowboy to one of Hollywood's top movie cowboys. By age 21, he was a western star for Republic Pictures.

The film company will be headquartered at the Glade Valley School campus. Filming will be done in several parts of the county including Whitehead, Laurel Springs, Piney Creek, and parts of New River according to Burgiss.

So Hollywood, move over - Alleghany may be the star of the new trend toward shooting on location movie hits - who knows?

MBR

On the set of *Dark Power* (L to R): Sammy Fulp, Lash LaRue, and producer/director Phil Smoot.

On the set of *Alien Outlaw* (L to R): Sunset Carson, Kari Anderson, and Lash.

Reprinted from *Roanoke Times and World-News*, May 3, 1986

Famed 'oater' actors enjoy Knoxville limelight

by Paul Dellinger
Staff Writer

Lash LaRue, a Saturday matinee western star a few decades ago, predicts that some of the old "oaters' from those days will be coming back in computerized color.

"They won't have to pay any of the actors over. They'll just put 'em in color and give 'em to you again. It's coming," the bullwhip-wielding star said during an April visit to Knoxville, Tenn.

LaRue broke tradition with the white-hatted good guys by dressing entirely in black in his oaters—slang for a western "horse opera".

He was among those attending the Riders of the Silver Screen Film Caravan at the former World's Fair site in Knoxville. Others visiting with the old and new western fans included Sunset Carson, Jock Mahoney, Dub "Cannonball" Taylor, Peggy Stewart, and Johnny Crawford, who played Chuck Connors' son on TV's "The Rifleman."

Also on hand was Pierce Lyden, who used to earn his acting salary by regularly getting shot or beaten up by the likes of "Wild Bill" Elliott or Johnny Mack Brown. "After all these nice people, I don't know how you can applaud for an old bad guy like me," he told an enthusiastic audience.

LaRue and Carson recently made some movies in North Carolina that will probably be released soon.

LaRue is as blunt about one of them, "The Dark Power," as he used to be when manhandling outlaws. "I didn't care for it." he said. "Do I have to talk about it?"

He and Carson were more enthusiastic about "Alien Outlaws," in which visitors from space look on Earth as a hunting preserve and the star—a young woman taught in the movie to handle firearms by no less an expert then Carson—must defend herself against them.

Taylor, who developed his Georgia cracker "Cannonball" role in films with Elliott, Tex Ritter, Charles Starrett, and Jimmy Wakely, has changed little from his movie appearance except for the whitening of his hair.

Buck Taylor, his son, was also on hand. Buck was one of the regulars on TV's "Gunsmoke," playing Newly O'Brien, and worked more recently in "General Hospital." His character on that soap opera has been killed off, but he continues to act in it because the scripts call for his character to keep appearing in a young woman's dreams.

For Carson, who wore a gunbelt and brace of six-guns from some of his movies, the autograph sessions and meeting the fans were painful chores. He had suffered a crushed hip that three operations had not yet put right, and was in pain much of the time—but he never lost his smile.

"They're going to have to start calling me 'Hoppy,'" he joked as he limped across the stage during one appearance.

Mahoney, who got into the movie business as a stunt man for actors like Charles Starrett, went on to play leading men in westerns — he and Stewart co-starred in the 1950 serial, "Cody of the Pony Express" — as well as bigger-budgeted films including two movies in which he played Tarzan.

Lash LaRue takes a short break from his autograph-signing session.

He visited the historic Tennessee Theatre in downtown Knoxville, a grand old house, complete with an onstage organ player to warm up audiences before the movies.

"I love these old theaters," he said. "The new theaters, excuse the expression, are kind of crappy. And some of the movies are in the same vein."

But Mahoney said CBS has gotten the rights to produce some of the popular novels by Louis L'Armour, "so we're going to get some damned good westerns."

The old B-westerns have been rediscovered in the past decade, with conventions featuring the surviving stars cropping up around the country and the shows themselves being rerun on cable networks.

"I wish Fuzzy could've been around long enough to see how long we lasted," LaRue said, referring to his movie sidekick played by comedian Al St. John.

Reprinted from *Greensboro News and Record*, May 7, 1986

Meeting favorite old-time cowboy gives mother special link to past

by Jerry Bledsoe

Elma Ramsey couldn't believe it when she looked up from her work to see her friend Olene Coble at the door with a man dressed in black.

"I bet you don't know who this is." Olsen said, as Elma opened the door.

"Oh, yes, I do, too."

Elma would have known even if she hadn't seen the long white Cadillac convertible parked out front with the license tag reading "1-Lash."

After all, Olene had said that she might bring Lash LaRue, the old-time cowboy movie star, to meet her one of these days. But Elma thought it was just talk.

Elma has a little alterations shop in the side of her small house on Sheridan Road in north Greensboro, and she's been doing work for Olene so long that the two have become friends. More than a year ago Olene told her about meeting Lash LaRue at a cookout at Belews Creek when Lash was here filming a movie he made in the area.

Olene and Lash became friends, and several times in the past year, Lash has been to Greensboro to visit her.

Shortly after one of those trips, Olene was talking to Elma about Lash, and Elma said, "You know, my baby boy wouldn't miss a one of his movies if he could help it."

Elma went to get a picture to show Olene. It was made 35 years ago when James Howard Ramsey, the youngest of her four children, was 12 years old. It shows him standing on the edge of a field, dressed in a black cowboy suit and hat, fancy boots, twin holsters, his hands on his six-guns, his feet spread apart.

James Howard loved Lash LaRue. The family lived then on a farm near Stokesdale, and the nearest theater was in Madison. Cowboy movies were shown there every Saturday, and James Howard always begged to go and see them, especially when a Lash LaRue movie was showing.

That was his hero, Elma explained. "He imitated him in every way. He dressed like him. He tried to walk like him."

He even made himself a bullwhip that he went around popping. "Oh, he tried to snap that little whip," his mother said.

Several months after that photo was made, on Nov. 12, 1951, just a couple of months after James Howard's 13th birthday, he got into a car with his older brother, Jay Lee, and a couple of other boys to go to a country store. The car crashed into the gas pumps at the store and overturned. James Howard was thrown out.

A friend came to tell Elma and drove her to the old Piedmont Memorial Hospital in downtown Greensboro, where all four boys had been taken.

James Howard's neck was broken and when Elma finally got to see him, a doctor was leaning over him, holding his face saying, "James, can you hear me? James?"

"I said, 'Let me speak to him.'" Elma remembers. "I said, 'James Howard, honey.' He said, 'Mother, mother,' and they were the last words he ever uttered." She still cries at the memory.

That picture of James in his cowboy suit became Elma's most treasured possession, and she went to get it when she started telling Lash how much her son admired him.

Lash took the yellowing snapshot and looked at it silently for a long moment, then excused himself and went out to the car. He came back carrying a photograph of himself in his heyday, dressed in black, hat pushed back, legs apart, his hands on his six-shooters.

"He was astonished at the similarities." says Elma.

Lash stayed for an hour. Elma told him all about James Howard. He told her about the movies he made. He autographed his photograph for her and gave her a color picture of himself with Roy Rogers and Dale Evans and a lot of other old-time movie cowboys made at a recent taping of a TV show to be shown this fall.

As Lash was getting ready to leave, Elma said, "It's a pity James Howard couldn't have been here to meet you as much as he adored you."

"I think he knows," Lash said.

Lash returned to his home in California Monday, leaving behind something far more special than photographs with Elma.

"I tell you," she says, "it was just like somebody had brought my son back to me for a little while."

Reprinted from *Greensboro News & Record*, August 28, 1986

Cowboy Lash LaRue is looking to lasso more than memories

by Jim Jenkins

Lash LaRue's voice growled with the earliness of the hour and the legacy of too many Pall Malls.

The silver hair and the white beard were made lighter and more striking against the trademark black shirt, pants, hat, belt and boots. Lash LaRue was the Man in Black when Johnny Cash was still picking cotton in Arkansas.

He was Rambo before Stallone had biceps, or even long pants.

Didn't need guns and grenades and long knives, either.

Just that whip.

He didn't have the whip on him this morning. He was in Greensboro to promote his upcoming Saturday appearance at the House of Stars, a museum of sorts to LaRue and the other old-time big screen cowboys, five miles south of Madison on U.S. 220. LaRue will be there all day.

But he probably won't do much with the whip.

"My eyes," he said. "I don't have the depth perception that you have in youth. I used to bring it right up next to a kid's mouth. But I wouldn't try to do that anymore. It's like a razor, you know. It can lay a man's arm open."

Time was, Lash LaRue made $2,000 a week and had a piece of the action on his movies, the action-packed adventures like "Stage to Mesa City," in which—though dressed in black—LaRue would knock off the bad guys by taking the guns out of their hands with the whip.

Of all the B-movie Western stars of the 1940s and '50s, LaRue is not the best looking, the best singer, the most wholesome, the most heroic—but he may be the most enduring.

His schedule is filled with personal appearances at Western film conventions and promotions. His glossies signed with a flourish generally do not last out the day. People who grew up on him and the kids they raised gather round him wherever he goes.

"CBN (Christian Broadcast Network) bought all my movies," he said. So they show them quite a bit. So the audience isn't limited to the over-35 set anymore."

And LaRue is seen quite a bit in North Carolina, where he now lives most of the time. He maintains a home in California, but operates out of Sanford. "I've always been in and out of the Carolinas a lot," he said. "In fact, my movie production company (from the old days) started in Charlotte."

He also has made two movies—"Dark Power" and "Alien Outlaw"—in the last two years, both out of a Kernersville production office.

"They're supposed to show "Dark Power" around Asheboro," LaRue said, but he regrets the lack of attention the films have gotten. "When we started it, we got a full page in People magazine, things like that. But I don't know. I always say that I'm wondering if they're waiting for me to drop dead or something."

LaRue rode his horse and his life fast in his younger days (he's now in his mid-60s) and reckons that a hearty constitution must be what carried him through it.

"I guess I've got the heart of a horse," he said. "I've never had any trouble. It'll probably all happen at once and I'll just drop over."

He refuses to talk much about the wild days or to say how many times he was married, though he acknowledges that he went through much of the big money he made.

"All I'll say is that if you get married more than once, you don't end up with anything," he said. "You can't make a silk purse out of a sow's ear, and I guess I'm a sow's ear. But it isn't until about 60 that a man gets a little sense."

LaRue would like to start his own touring show with Western action and comedy, but wants a backer—"a soft drink company or a candy company"—to support it.

"And I'm not sure I could get people to come away from their television sets to see it," he said.

The attempt to do something new—away from the black-and-white film conventions and the nostalgia for old-time cowboys—has always seemed to fizzle.

"I've been trying to get that whip out of my hand for 30 years," LaRue said. "But you get typecast, and that's what people want. I wish I could try something with real acting. But Westerns, they're not coming back."

Lash arrived right on time for a guest appearance at the House of Stars memorabilia store. (August 30, 1986)

The kids also knew Lash, thanks to TV reruns and videotapes. (August 30, 1986)

Lash with fan club president Barbara Arnette at the House of Stars. (August 30, 1986)

Bobby Atkins, recording artist and 5-string banjo wizard, met Lash LaRue at the House of Stars.

Reprinted from *The Messenger*, September 3, 1986.

Lash LaRue

Actor Can't Quit After 75 Movies

by Neil Purdy

Stardom.

The "silver screen" makes stars bigger than life. And they have a certain "something" that awes even those who have never seen their films.

That could explain why children from two to twelve were awed with the chance to see Western star Lash LaRue at Don and Noreen Key's "House of Stars" on U.S. 220 south of Madison, though probably only a few had seen his old "horse operas" on Saturday morning television.

Or it could have been Lash's own attitude toward the children: he loved them.

The middle-aged to elderly approached him for autographs and commented on his Hollywood films. LaRue was friendly to all and shared life experiences with his peers, but it was to the children that he showed the most enthusiasm Saturday.

One little boy was overheard asking LaRue if he should say his prayers.

"You say them, pardner!" said Lash. "When I was about your age, I prayed to be a cowboy, and when I grew up that's what happened."

"My first was 'Song of Old Wyoming,' and it was the first film to break the monopoly Technicolor had at the time."

Pinning him down on chronology was difficult.

"How old are you?"

"I'm legal," said LaRue.

"There are about three dates published on my birthday, but they don't know. I'm not saying. It's nice to be older than you look."

He does admit, though, that he began in the movies in 1945, and it was in 1946 before he was awarded a starring contract. From 1948 he did movies for Western Adventure Productions, a movie corporation put together in Charlotte.

How did he get into the acting profession in the first place?

"I was in California in law school, wanting to be an attorney, but I had a serious speech impediment. One of the things I did to work on that," said LaRue, whose speech is a flawless baritone, "was to take dramatics."

"But I didn't know what good acting was until I got on the road."

Like most actors, once he got the "bug" LaRue lived his life "on the road."

As throughout his career, he's still traveling. The day before he was at the "House of Stars" he appeared and signed autographs in Tampa, Fla. His next stop was to be the following day in Roanoke, Va. On Sept. 6, he is to be at the "Collector's Dream World" in Pigeon Forge, Tenn.

Since his Hollywood days, LaRue has acted in television and movies as frequently as possible—among his guest star appearances being his performance on Hugh O'Brian's "Wyatt Earp" television series.

IN PERSON

SATURDAY, AUGUST 30

AT THE "HOUSE OF STARS"

5 Miles South of Madison on U.S. 220

LASH LARUE

"KING OF THE BULLWHIP"

BRING THE KIDS — APPEARING 10:00 A.M. TO 4:00 P.M. — BRING YOUR CAMERA

WHILE AT THE HOUSE OF STARS VISITING LASH YOU MAY LOOK OVER THE SELECTION OF MOVIE COLLECTIBLES, PHOTOS, VIDEO TAPES, ROCK AND MOVIE POSTERS, MAGAZINES, RECORDS, BOOKS, POSTCARDS, PRINTED T SHIRTS, BUTTONS, NOVELTIES AND COWBOY COLLECTIBLES.

DON'T MISS THIS OPPORTUNITY
TO MEET AND TALK WITH THIS MOVIE COWBOY LEGEND

With the black cowboy outfit and his trademark whip, Lash didn't have to add he'd made it as a Hollywood cowboy. But a cowboy's a cowboy, right?

Of his career, he said later, "I've made 75 pictures. Some were gang movies, some detectives, a lot of character roles. But it was in my 35 Westerns that I made a name. I was seemingly a natural for Westerns."

"In one of the takes, I beat O'Brian on the draw!" LaRue recalled, "Hugh couldn't believe that."

How do present movies compare with those produced during the "Golden Age" of Hollywood?

"Technically, the business has gotten better, but the stories leave a lot to be desired now," LaRue said.

"They think they have to show blood 'n guts, but if they showed more story they'd have better pictures. What you see now is just scenes tied together with exciting music."

"Bill Cosby has showed, though, that you don't have to be nasty in order to be popular, and people like Waylon Jennings, Johnny Cash, and Willie Nelson are now making better pictures and will leave a permanent mark on the industry."

"Johnny Cash is one man who's wrestled with the devil and won," he said.

Now at age "X" will he continue to act?

"I expect to act for the rest of my life," said LaRue. "I can't quit now."

Reprinted from *Roanoke Times and World-News*, September 10, 1986

Lash LaRue to visit the Grandin Theatre

by Paul Dellinger

Lash LaRue, whose bullwhip and black outfit made bad guys blanch in a string of westerns between 1945 and 1951, will visit the Grandin Theatre Saturday during an all day movie program.

The films will include two of LaRue's movies and two others featuring Charles Starrett as the Durango Kid and Allan "Rocky" Lane.

The free program will run from 10 a.m. to about 4 p.m. It is being sponsored by the Western Film Club of Roanoke.

Nate Booth, whose "Old Prospector" guise has been popular at B-Western film festivals in various states, also will be on hand along with dealers selling items related to old-time movies.

Bob Carman, co-author of a series of illustrated books on western movie stars, is coordinating the event. Carman, who moved to Roanoke from New York last year, has published books on the westerns of Roy Rogers, Sunset Carson, Rex Allen, Monte Hale and Starrett's Durango Kid series.

Carman said the "Saturday matinee" at the Grandin could become a monthly event, if there is enough interest.

The old movies have enjoyed a revival of sorts in recent years, on cable television channels like CBN and TBS and at various film festivals where they are shown on small screens.

"I'd love to walk into a movie theater and see a B-Western on the big screen," Carman said, which was why he set up the program at the Grandin. "I think the big screen's going to help a lot."

The scheduled films are "Fighting Vigilantes" with LaRue and Al "Fuzzy" St. John at 10:30 a.m., "Rustlers on Horseback" with Lane at noon, "Galloping Thunder" with Starrett at 1:30 p.m., and "King of the Bullwhip" at 3 p.m.

"King," released in 1950, is probably the best known of LaRue's more than 20 westerns. It co-stars St. John, Jack Holt, Tom Neal, Dennis Moore, and George Lewis, and features a masked bull-whip-wielding bandit leader who has a whip duel with LaRue at the film's climax.

LaRue will appear on stage between films and talk about them. Carman said the program also will include some cartoons and other short films.

LaRue began his career in westerns in 1945 with "Song of Old Wyoming." He portrayed the Cheyenne Kid, a shady character working for the bad guys until he discovers that the woman ranch owner they are victimizing is his mother. The movie ends with him changing sides in time to sacrifice himself to rout the outlaws.

The star of the movie was singer Eddie Dean, but LaRue's portrayal drew most of the fan mail. He co-starred in two more films with Dean and then was given his own series.

By then, LaRue had established his image. Working against the white-hatted hero cliché, he dressed entirely in black and even rode a black horse.

After low-budget western movies lost ground to television in the 1950s, LaRue appeared in such TV shows as "Wyatt Earp," "Judge Roy Bean" and others.

His career later went downhill, the low point coming in the late 1960s when he was arrested for vagrancy with just 35 cents in his pocket. His contact with an evangelist led to his religious rededication and appearances around the country in programs aimed at rounding up souls for the Lord.

He has even made some more movies, including "Alien Outlaw," which was filmed not far from Southwest Virginia in a section of North Carolina.

Reprinted from *Greensboro News & Record*, December 22, 1986.

LaRue fans to hit the trail for N.C. bash

Lash LaRue's films were always set way out West, but the site of a planned "National Day of Appreciation" for the legendary movie cowboy is a mighty long ride from Hollywood.

The event, expected to attract Western film buffs from around the country, will be held in Raleigh, a town known more for college students and state senators than saddles, sagebrush and shootouts.

But Lash LaRue's links to the Tar Heel state have been long and lasting, his mark left firmly engraved here by more than Saturday morning matinee memories of a black-garbed figure wielding a bullwhip.

LaRue says he was a bit taken aback, even a little embarrassed, when he first learned that fans and friends will gather Jan. 24 at a Raleigh hotel to honor him.

"I felt kinda funny about it...a little hesitant." LaRue said in a recent interview. "There sure are a lot more deserving people than I am."

But there are some folks in these parts who tend to take issue with LaRue on that last point.

That's because the Lash LaRue they know is perhaps the antithesis of the hard-edged, feisty character LaRue portrayed in a series of low-budget but highly successful Westerns filmed in the late 1940s.

To them, Lash LaRue is more than just a colorful crusty cinema cowpoke with a slightly checkered past.

He's the gracefully aging, white-bearded gent who frequents children's hospitals to bring a smile to youngsters who don't have a lot to smile about. And he's the same "good guy in black" who makes it a point to appear "at the drop of a hat" at the many Western film conventions and get-togethers held each year in North Carolina, a state that remains a hotbed of interest in Western movies the way they used to make them.

Ron Butler, vice chancellor of student affairs at N.C. State University in Raleigh is one of those heading up the appreciation day effort. He says accolades for LaRue are long overdue.

"He's done so much for so long, especially when it comes to efforts to preserve old-time Western movies," Butler said.

The appreciation day came about when Siler City's Milo Holt moved his quarterly Old Time Western Film Club meeting for January to Raleigh and joined forces with the Raleigh Chapter of the Western Film Preservation Society, Inc., headedThe by Ed Wyatt.

Holt and Wyatt said the thinking behind the gathering is that "We feel time has come to honor our friend, Lash LaRue, who has done so much to keep B-Western films alive for future generations. We are asking B-Western fans everywhere to join us in this special celebration."

LaRue's ties to North Carolina are many. In the late 1940s and early 1950s he made a series of films for a production company based in Charlotte and headed by former Asheboro businessman J. Francis White. His public appearances in the state with his former sidekick, the late Al "Fuzzy" St. John, were frequent.

Last year, LaRue was chosen by Kernersville filmmaker Phil Smoot, formerly of Asheboro, to star in two adventure pictures filmed in North Carolina.

"It's about time someone honored Lash." Smoot said. "You know, he was one of the few cowboy stars who was really a very good actor. In many ways it's unfortunate that he got typecast in his cowboy role."

LaRue says he continues to make public appearances because "it helps keep me young...younger than I am old.

"Age is a philosophical trap, you see, and doing things helps me beat it."

So he brushes aside the accolades except to say he thinks Lash LaRue Day is a good idea only "if it will help me to help others.

"But I'm not gonna go around and crow about it."

He has one regret about the appreciation day.

"You know, I do kind of wish Fuzzy could be around for this appreciation day thing."

Reprinted from *Raleigh Times*, January 23, 1987

The Lash laugh

The King of the Bullwhip finally gets his place in the sun(set)

by Debbie Moose, *Times* staff writer

Whatever happened to the days when men were men, women were women, and a horse was a man's best friend?

Those were the days of the B-Western movies in the '30s and '40s, and their passing left a tall pair of boots to fill.

John Wayne filled them for a while, although he was allowed to grow old and have mid-life crises on the silver screen (we like our heroes young and uncomplicated.) Clint Eastwood has tried to fill them, but lately he has preferred to be a hard-talking Marine instead of a white-hatted good guy.

Those holding out for a hero, B-Western style, can meet one of the few that are left on Saturday at the "National Day of Appreciation for Lash LaRue" sponsored by the Raleigh chapter of the Western Film Preservation Society and the Old Time Western Film Club of Siler City. (Yes, that's national.)

Besides a luncheon honoring LaRue, who lives in Sanford, and displays of memorabilia, the day will include a public showing at the Imperial Theater in Cary of his classic "King of the Bullwhip" (1951).

LaRue made about 35 B-Westerns from the 1930s to the '50s, and his career spanned the golden age of the form. B-Westerns typically were shot in three to four days on budgets that would be hardly enough to build R2D2 today. But their humble origins didn't matter to kids who packed the picture palaces—they devoured the fast action and simple plots.

"The urge to recall those thrilling (and innocent) days of yesteryear is one reason the old horse operas are still riding the range," said Ron Butler of the Raleigh Western Film Preservation Society.

"For those of us who grew up with them, it's nostalgia on our part," said Butler, who is associate vice chancellor for student affairs at N.C. State University when he's not scanning the sagebrush. "You can escape a little reality. They're totally unreal, but fun. And they had a pretty good message."

The message, whether Gene Autry belted out in a song or the Lone Ranger carried it on Silver, was: Good will always win over evil, and it will win without so much as losing its white hat.

There was a moral to every tumbleweed tale, LaRue said from his office in Sanford. "The good guy always wins, although he might get into some trouble," he said. "And they represent a period that we look back on and wish was here again."

Although LaRue's movies fit the themes, he cut a different image from the traditional good guys. Dressed all in black and wielding a long bullwhip, he was something else. "You could not quite put your finger on it," James Horwitz wrote on his book on B-Westerns, *They Went Thataway*. "Lash LaRue seemed to hint at things (kids) did not yet know anything about."

LaRue said that in most of his movies he was a bad guy who turns good. But even reformed bad guys don't always get a reward—in "Song of Old Wyoming," his character straightens himself out but gets killed for his trouble.

LaRue (who won't tell his age) said a new movie starring him, "The Dark Power," will premiere Feb. 13 in Greensboro.

The B-Western hasn't ridden into the sunset, although you might not recognize some of its new costumes. "The laser-packing spacemen of "Star Wars" could have ridden straight off the range," Calhoun said. "And Darth Vader may have had a light saber strapped to his hip instead of a pearl-handled revolver, but he still wore black."

But why haven't new Westerns which try to recreate the old B-movie excitement, like "Silverado," been big smashes? "We've grown up," Calhoun said, "and lost our innocence."

But you can still see the old greats ride again. The traditional values in classic Westerns appealed to the CBN Cable Network, said Earl Weirich, public relations director for the network, which is owned by Christian Broadcasting in Virginia Beach, Va. CBN offers classic Westerns on "Sunday at the Westerns" at 2 p.m. Sundays and "Western Theater" at 5 p.m. Sundays.

Besides the shows on CBN, the Nashville Network has brought back Roy Rogers and wife Dale Evans (whose real name was Fanny Butts, according to Horwitz's book). They're back in the saddle again to host their old movies on "Happy Trails Theatre" at 11 a.m., 5 p.m. and 1 a.m. Saturdays. The network also has "Tumbleweed Theatre," hosted by Western singers Riders in the Sky, at 1 p.m. Monday-Friday. Cinemax schedules classic Westerns in its regular lineup.

So Trigger may be stuffed and mounted, but the white hats are not forgotten—the men (as touted by a poster for an old Ken Maynard movie) "who ride with their stirrups long and their holsters handy, who deal across the top of the table and shoot from the hip."

"Lash LaRue Appreciation Day," Saturday, 10 a.m. - 6 p.m., Ramada Inn Raleigh - South at Highway 55 and U.S. 1, free except charge for lunch. "King of the Bullwhip," 11 a.m., Imperial Theatre, $1 for general public.

The following two articles are reprinted from *The Cary News*, January 28, 1987

Fans come to see fastest Lash

by James Hyatt, staff writer

About 250 people gathered Saturday in Apex to show B-Western star Lash LaRue their appreciation for making long-ago Saturday afternoons so enjoyable.

The National Lash LaRue Appreciation Day was held at the Apex Ramada Inn from 10 a.m. to 6 p.m. The program was co-sponsored by the Raleigh Chapter of the Western Film Preservation Society, Inc., and the Old Time Western Film Club of Siler City.

In the 1940s and '50s, LaRue was one of the most popular Western film stars. He made about 35 movies, most of them with his on-screen sidekick and off-screen friend, Al "Fuzzy" St. John. St. John died several years ago.

Fans of LaRue gathered at the motel to meet the Hollywood hero and buy autographed pictures of him in action, buy B-Western movie memorabilia from collectors and watch old films.

The majority of fans were middle-aged men, many of whom dressed in cowboy gear in honor of Lash and the vision of the American West that he represented on celluloid.

The day's main event was a special showing of LaRue's 1951 film, "King of the Bullwhip," at the Imperial Cinema IV Theaters in Cary.

The showing drew between 350 and 400 people, many of them couples with children too young to know who LaRue is but old enough to appreciate a good shoot-'em-up.

"It was a big day," said Ron Butler of the Western Film Preservation Society. "Everything went super well. Everybody bought popcorn and went in to watch a movie just like 30 years ago."

Before the film started, LaRue gave the crowd a brief demonstration of his prowess with his trademark whip, then told the group he appreciated their enthusiasm.

"You know, I had a lot of fun making pictures," he said. "But I don't think I've ever enjoyed my career any more than I have in the last few years. I feel very flattered about the special attention that the Western Film Preservation Society has given me. I wish Fuzzy was around to see how long it lasted."

Still, Saturday's show was just an echo of the past, when an appearance by LaRue could pack local theaters.

"This is not quite like it used to be back in the old days when they had 700-seat houses," LaRue told the group at the theater. "Those were good days. Remember when the big screen was going and all those Saturday afternoon matinees?"

After the film ended, fans trekked back to Apex to honor LaRue during a special presentation.

LaRue, who was dressed in his trademark black outfit, was presented a check and a scrapbook filled with letters from fans across the country, Butler said.

"Those letter-writing fans included Gov. James G. Martin and Waylon Jennings," Butler said.

A special preview of two films starring LaRue, "The Dark Power" and "Alien Outlaw" were shown by producer Phil Smoot of Triad Motion Pictures.

"The Dark Power" is scheduled to premier Feb. 13 in Greensboro," LaRue said.

"No plans have been made for the premier of "Alien Outlaw", but the film is scheduled to be released sometime this year," Butler said.

LaRue: King of bullwhip

by James Hyatt, staff writer

Many fans of Lash LaRue didn't get a chance to talk to the real man behind the bullwhip Saturday.

Many people preferred to tell the Western star how much LaRue the actor meant to them during their childhood, how he stood for justice and The American Way in a time when moral issues seemed black and white, like the films of the day.

His fans' tendency to talk instead of to listen is understandable, because during their childhoods LaRue's character stood tall and spoke firmly.

LaRue usually wore a badge and was kind to women, children and horses. He was brave and resolute when dealing with the bad guys, resorting first to his whip and then to his fists, using his pistol only when he had no other choice.

He was a 40 foot high father figure who appeared every Saturday morning to reassure his audience of children that everything would turn out for the best.

Even after five children and "a whole bunch of grandchildren," the desire to represent all the best parts of fatherhood still stays with LaRue.

"I never had a daddy," LaRue said in an interview conducted during a break in Saturday's program. "I was a widow's son. She kept looking for a man to help me, and I'd run them out. I didn't want them around. So the only one I had to look up to was people like John Wayne.

"I want to be the kind of a daddy that I never had. I had a little boy one time come up and ask me on the road, he says 'Are you married?' and at that time I wasn't. So he sold me a bill of goods on his mama. Now he wanted me for a daddy and that's the highest compliment a guy can pay another guy."

His respect for Wayne is evident in the way he talks about him and the friendship that never quite developed.

"We met many times," he said. "We didn't get as well acquainted as I'd like to have had. I wrote him a letter when he was in the hospital and I told him I never knew my dad, but if I had..I'd wish my dad had been a lot like him. And I think that says a lot."

LaRue also has a lighter side, even admitting that he didn't know how to use a bullwhip when his film career started.

"I lied to get a part in a picture," he said with a broad smile.

The producer and writer of the picture had a secretary that he relied on. "I knew her and when I went into his office, he didn't talk to me at all. He said, 'Well, he looks the part, if he can act.' I said, Mr. Tandy, I'm probably the best actor that's ever been in your office.

"He looked at her, smiled and said 'Well, he's either good or he's nuts.'"

The producer told LaRue he was looking for someone who could handle a whip. Even though he didn't have the experience, LaRue assured the producer he knew his way around a bullwhip and the rest is B movie history.

"I went out and rented a 20 foot whip and beat myself to death trying to learn how to handle that sucker," he said. "I couldn't find anybody that ever threw a whip. I hurt myself so bad I had stripes on my back.

"He said... 'Don't worry about how good you are with it, just be able to get it out in front of you and make it look like it was easy for you to do.' So I knew I could do that and that damn whip beat me every time I threw it. And each time I threw it hard enough to get it out there, it hit me again.

"We were three days into the picture and I had stripes on my back and the whip hanging on my belt. I hadn't been called to use it but I'd been in some scenes. (The producer) is tickled to death with what I've got on picture..so he says 'How would you like to do three pictures at three times the money you're making?'

"I said, 'Hey, that sounds good.' But then I said, 'Bob, I've got to tell you something. I can't use that whip.' His face drops to here, I said, 'Wait a minute. You doubted I could act, so I just acted like I could. That isn't lying.'

"I pulled up my shirt and showed him what I did to myself trying to learn. He thought it was the funniest thing he'd ever heard. So he hired somebody to come out and work with me, and in between scenes I really worked. By the time the picture was over, I was well on my way because I wanted it so bad."

LaRue, who has made over 35 films, got his big break as "The Cheyenne Kid". His popularity in that role lead to his first feature, "Law of the Lash". He then dropped his first name, Al, in favor of Lash, a name he has kept ever since.

He refuses to tell anyone how old he is, saying he doesn't want his age to limit him personally or professionally.

"Age is a psychological trap," LaRue said, "If I started thinking about how old I was, I wouldn't be able to get up in the morning."

Known as the whip-wielding cowboy in black, LaRue finds himself in the odd position of being famous without being in front of the public for several years.

"I'm kind of a household name but I've got nothing to sell but me," he said. "I'd like to be a PR man for a candy company. I think I could to a good job for them.

"I've got an idea for a show that I think would work out real well. It would be me as a story-teller talking about the old days and then do flashbacks on my films, which I think would be a good personal touch. A rapport with the kids is what I'd like to get. I feel like I've been rehearsing 40 years for one speech and I'm not booked yet to make it."

The message LaRue wants to deliver in his speech "has little to do with his career and everything to do with his faith in God," he said.

"Nobody would have ever picked me to carry a message, but He did," LaRue said. "I think we've been caught up in a circle of distortion and destruction."

Reprinted from *The Courier-Tribune*, February 20, 1988

Two Lash LaRues' trails finally cross

by Bob Williams, news editor

CHARLOTTE - When the trails of two good guys, both named Lash LaRue, finally crossed again after 40 years, it was as if some sort of cowpoke prophecy had been fulfilled.

But when the two men were reunited at a gun show here last Saturday, it was no surprise that former cowboy movie star Al "Lash" LaRue didn't really remember J.R. "Lash" LaRue, his namesake and biggest fan.

After all, the last time they'd had eyes on each other was in 1948.

Al "Lash" LaRue was at the height of his fame then, a black-garbed, bullwhip-wielding figure who rode roughshod and larger than life across the silver screen and straight into the cowboy fantasies of youngsters all across America.

J.R. LaRue was one of those youngsters...just a face in the crowd at one of the hundreds of personal appearances the cowboy star made in countless towns, small and large, in those days.

But J.R. LaRue, now 47, never got over the day Lash LaRue came to his hometown of Metropolis, Ill. (pop: 1,300), for a stage show. Even though he was just 7 years old, that long ago Saturday morning still "seems like yesterday." It was the day that, because they shared the same last name, his hero singled him out of the audience and asked him to come up on stage.

And J.R. LaRue became the envy of every kid in town by being brave enough to hold aloft a piece of paper that was quickly shredded by Lash LaRue's flailing bullwhip.

After that, everyone started referring to young J.R. LaRue simply as "Lash." The name stuck. In fact, J.R. LaRue adopted it, made it his own in homage to his hero. To this day that's what folks call him and it's the name that appears on his business cards.

His business cards also say that he is now a "dealer in fine firearms" and operator of a gun shop in Portsmouth, NH., the place he finally settled down after spending 22 years in the U.S. Air Force.

And it was one of those business cards, coupled with a bit of coincidence and a smidgen of luck, that would bring him, 40 years later, back into contact with his cowboy hero.

Over the years J.R. LaRue kept tabs on the comings and goings of Lash LaRue through newspaper and magazine clippings. In fact, he compiled a huge, three-ring binder filled with LaRue articles. "I kept track of him through the good times and bad."

He knew that Lash LaRue had continued to keep up a rigorous schedule of public appearances, especially in the South, but somehow their paths never seemed to cross.

"And I really wanted to see my old hero one more time."

His opportunity to do just that was waiting in the wings. The catalyst was a chance encounter two weeks ago with Wil Scotten, a western movie buff from Asheboro.

Scotten, who is active in the North Carolina-based Western Film Preservation Society and curator of the N.C. Department of History's Mobile Western Museum, showed up at J.R. LaRue's booth at a gun show in Greensboro and they began negotiating over the price of a weapon.

"We couldn't get together on the price of the gun but I decided to take one of his business cards and noticed that it said his name was 'Lash LaRue.'" Scotten recalled.

"I told him he was the second Lash LaRue I'd met and he proceeded to tell me the story about appearing on stage with the real Lash all those years ago and how folks have called him Lash ever since.

"I could tell by the way his face lit up that he really was a big fan of Lash's," said Scotten, who had already begun to form the germ of an idea.

He knew the real Lash LaRue well since LaRue often makes personal appearances at functions and film conventions sponsored by the Western Film Preservation Society.

And he thought it might be "fun" to get Lash, the gun dealer, together again with Lash, the cowboy hero.

J.R. LaRue planned to have a booth at a big gun show in Charlotte, scheduled for Feb. 13. He contacted Lash LaRue through his business manager and LaRue agreed that, on the day of the show, he would travel to Charlotte from Spartanburg, S.C., to meet his biggest fan.

"Lash was more than willing to do it...said he thought it was a cute idea," Scotten recalled.

When Lash LaRue walked up to J.R. LaRue's booth at the Charlotte gun show last weekend, the years seemed to suddenly wash away.

The two men immediately launched into animated conversation as if 40 minutes, not 40 years, separated them. Both immediately noticed that they even resembled each other a bit...at least both sported graying beards.

And Lash LaRue wanted to know if, all those years ago, his namesake had been scared when he held up that piece of paper to the untender mercies of the bullwhip.

"Hell, yes, I was scared," J.R. LaRue answered.

Lash LaRue didn't doubt it. "Why when I used to do that bullwhip act, I had mothers running down the aisles of the theaters trying to rescue their sons. But I always hit the paper, never the kid."

Then he asked if the theater in J.R. LaRue's hometown had been packed that day back in '48.

"Sure was," J.R. LaRue said. "Packed to the rafters."

Lash LaRue nodded and smiled slightly. "They always were in those days," he said, remembering.

Then J.R. LaRue recalled that his old hero had autographed a photo for him on that long-ago day and that it had become his most cherished possession. He hung onto it for years, up until he joined the Air Force. That's when his nephew nabbed the photo, posted it on an outhouse wall and proceeded to shoot it full of holes.

"That's about the only time I can recall one of my photos being used for target practice." Lash LaRue said with a laugh, then promptly autographed some new photos, and a comic book, for his long-time fan.

Other folks in attendance at the gun show were beginning to figure out that cowboy legend Lash LaRue was in attendance and there was suddenly something of a clamor for autographs.

J.R. LaRue watched intently as Lash LaRue signed photos for a line of fans - many of them young boys - that had suddenly formed.

"I guess they've seen his movies on TV because they're sure too young to remember..." J.R. LaRue commented.

"You know, in my day we had real heroes, all the good guys like Lash, Roy Rogers, Gene Autry and all the others. Sometimes I wonder who today's kids have that they can look up to the way we looked up to those guys. I think that kind of hero worship made my generation grow up to be better people.

"Yeah, in those days when kids got together nobody wanted to play the bad guy."

About the time J.R. LaRue was saying that, Lash LaRue was signing autographs for a couple of preteenagers named Daniel and Jed. "Now you boys remember to study hard in school because you'll never amount to too much if you don't," he told them as they walked away.

A little while later, when asked about J.R. LaRue's comments concerning heroes, Lash LaRue thought for a long moment and said he does try to live up to the "good guy" image.

"In a way, it's a tough position to be in. But if that's the way folks see me...well I'm just as proud as I can be."

And Lash LaRue, who has recently been featured in two movies filmed in North Carolina and who remains in demand at public appearances, allowed that, back in the '40s, he certainly didn't expect his fame to last into the '80s.

"To tell you the truth, I didn't expect to live that long," he said.

J.R. LaRue was sort of hovering around the edges of that conversation and smiling a little bit. He didn't say it, but it was clear he was glad his old hero was still around.

The way J.R. LaRue figures it is that, even if there are two Lash LaRues, the town will always be big enough for both of them.

Lash is ready to crack the whip for flag and country. This picture was taken on the set of *Dark Power*.

Selected Bibliography

Brooks, Tim, and Earle Marsh. *The Complete Directory to Prime Time Network TV Shows 1946 - Present.* New York: Ballantine, 1979.

Dellinger, Paul. "King of the Bullwhip," *Under Western Skies*, No. 28, August 1984.

Dixon, Wheeler. *Producers Releasing Corporation.* North Carolina: McFarland Company, 1986.

LaHue, Kalton C. *Riders of the Range.* New York: Castle Books, 1973.

McClure, Arthur F., and Ken D. Jones. *Heroes, Heavies and Sagebrush.* New Jersey: A.S. Barnes and Company, Inc., 1972.

Miller, Don. *Hollywood Corral.* New York: Popular Library, 1976.

Rainey, Buck, assisted by Les Adams. "Lash & Fuzzy Too," *Under Western Skies,* No. 10, May 1980.

Rothel, David. *Those Great Cowboy Sidekicks.* North Carolina: Empire Publishing, Inc., 2001.

Wolmuth, Roger, "Hoist 'Em, Pards, Lash is Back," *People*, April 1, 1985.

About the Authors

Chuck Thornton

Hershel Edward "Chuck" Thornton was introduced to B Westerns by way of theatre re-issues and television in the late 1950s and early '60s in his hometown of Atlanta, Georgia. He began attending film festivals and collecting 16mm film and other B-Western movie memorabiliia in 1976. Having been inspired by the work of his friend Bob Carman on his excellent books, Chuck went on to compile three of his own: *The Western Adventures of Allan Lane*, *The Western Adventures of Lash LaRue* and *The Western Adventures of Tim Holt.* Presently, Mr. Thornton operates the family business, Herschel Thornton Mortuary, in Atlanta. He is married to the former Doretha Myers Martin and has two children, Gloria and Brandon, from his first marriage. In addition to enjoying the B Westerns, serials, etc. of a bygone era, Chuck also collects pro-wrestling memorabilia from the 1950s and '60s.

David Rothel *(Photo: Ken Taylor)*

David Rothel's lifelong fascination with show business began with frequent visits to his local movie theater, where he followed the adventures of his favorite Western heroes. He has since gone from youthful observer to performer, producer, director, teacher, and published authority on various aspects of popular entertainment (eleven books in twenty-five years). Mr. Rothel's most recent books include *Richard Boone, A Knight Without Armor in a Savage Land*; *The Gene Autry Book* and *The Roy Rogers Book*, both reference-trivia-scrapbooks; *An Ambush of Ghosts, A Personal Guide to Favorite Western Film Locations*, to which film historian Leonard Maltin devoted two *Entertainment Tonight* segments; and *Tim Holt*, a biography of the popular RKO Western star. Mr. Rothel has been married to his wife Nancy for over thirty-five years, has three children (Michael, Christopher, and Laura) and six grandchildren (Adam, Ryan, Nicholas, Alixandra, Alex, and Madison). Mr. Rothel's writing is characterized by thoroughness of research, warmth, wit, and understanding.

OTHER WESTERN PUBLICATIONS AVAILABLE FROM EMPIRE: